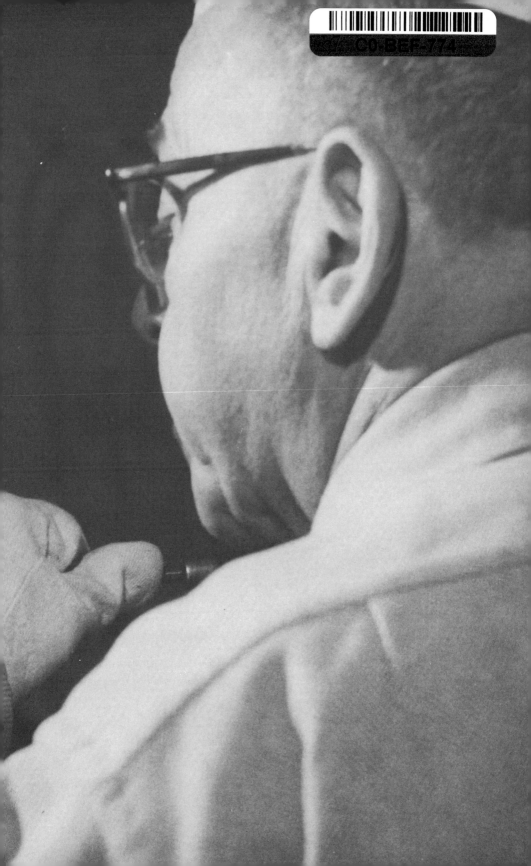

Life
Size

Life Size

an autobiography

by

Maurice Hexter

with the editorial cooperation of
Murray Teigh Bloom

PHOENIX PUBLISHING
West Kennebunk, Maine

Library of Congress Cataloging-in-Publication Data

Hexter, Maurice Beck, 1891-
  Life size: an autobiography / by Maurice B. Hex-
ter; with the editorial cooperation of Murray Teigh
Bloom.
     p. cm.
  ISBN 0-914659-45-6: $20.00
  1. Hexter, Maurice Beck, 1891- . 2. Jews — United
States — Biography. 3. Jews — United States —
Politics and government. 4. Jews — United States —
Charities. 5. Social workers — United States — Bio-
graphy. 6. Zionism. I. Bloom, Murray Teigh, 1916-
II. Title.
E184.J5H568 1990
973' .0492402 — dc20
  [B]   90-6802
                                                            CIP

Copyright 1990 by Maurice B. Hexter

Printed in the United States of America

Contents

Foreword

B Y ANY STANDARD, Maurice Hexter is a most extraordinary man. That he is ninety-eight years old and still vitally alive, mentally and physically, is remarkable in and of itself, even in the perspective of a father who died at ninety-nine, a sister at ninety-three, and a brother who died in an accident at ninety-four. It is mind-boggling when one considers Maurice's life has spanned the modern history of America from the Edwardian era of the late nineteenth century, the Spanish American War, the two World Wars, through the birth of the Nuclear Age and now the Computer Age. Most remarkable, is how richly he has filled his century.

From newsboy and pet of the prostitutes in the red-light district of Cincinnati, he matured to become an instructor of Economics at Harvard, a pioneer in Palestine deeply involved in the colonization movement, and eventually was among the founding fathers of Israel. He was so close to Israeli leaders that he was nominated for a ministry post in Ben-Gurion's first cabinet. Later, back home in New York, Maurice became a social worker nonpareil, architect of many major charities, including the enhancement of facilities and services at several major Jewish Federation hospitals in New York. Along life's way, he received no fewer than six honorary degrees. Last and certainly not least, Maurice became a sensitive, successful sculptor in stone, beginning at the tender age of fifty-nine and winning two gold medals from the National Sculpture Society. He is still never far from his hammer and stone.

Much of this is told in the following pages. What will perhaps be less evident is the warmth and caring about human beings that lies behind the apparent gruffness, and even shyness of Maurice's public image. Much as a careful study and understanding of Maurice's sculpture reveals the sensitivity and feeling reflected in his carvings of the rough hewn marble, so it has been the reward of his and those privileged others, who have truly known him, to understand and appreciate the underlying warmth and caring of Maurice as a human being.

Thus, the almost detached tone of the narrative in this book of his relationship with Marguerite conceals the underlying love and deep caring in their relationship that was evident to our family. We are referring especially to the tender care he gave Marguerite in her failing years and to his tears of agony as she faded from life. Even now, ten years after her passing, Maurice tells us how willingly he would give up his remaining years to have ten minutes with his beloved Marguerite.

So, too, we suspect, from what we know of Maurice, there must have been an underlying and enduring warmth and affection behind the formal facade of the relationships he had with his two principal mentors, Dr. Boris D. Bogen and Feliz Warburg. How revealing in this respect is Maurice's comment that it was only after several years in his relationship with Felix Warburg that Warburg called him "Maurice" rather than "Dr. Hexter"; and this by the very same Felix Warburg who wrote, as proxy for Maurice — at the time unreachable and unable to communicate from Palestine — a touching and sensitive letter to Marguerite on the occasion of Marge's birth in Milwaukee.

We ourselves had occasion, in a family visit in 1970 with David Ben-Gurion in his retirement at Sde-Bokar, to hear and sense at first-hand the warmth and affection that underlay the relationship between these two outwardly appearing blocks of granite. One need only observe Maurice's sculpture of Ben-Gurion, done from photographs taken by us on that occasion, to sense the depth of that feeling.

There is also the sensitivity, caring and mutual admiration that developed from the initially stormy relationship between Maurice and Leonard Block, whom we sometimes lovingly refer to as a "block off the old chip." And, equally revealing, are the infinitely tender and touching relationships between Maurice and the now failing centenarian, Lucy Moses, and almost-centenarian, Dr. Fishberg; the weekly visits to the former and the constant loving care which Maurice continues to give to his dear and invalided friend, Arthur Fishberg.

Probably more than any others, we of his family have witnessed the dedication with which he typically applied himself to his chosen life-long profession as a social worker, and to his endless interest and help as the head of our family. Witness Maurice's attention and tenderness toward Marge, which was circumscribed in her early years by the demands of his work and distant travel, but which now in less pressured years have permitted him to show his great warmth to both of us, our four children, our daughter-in-law, and Maurice's first great-grandchild, Kevin.

Finally, we note the mention at the end of the autobiography of the luncheons at the Harmonie Club at which Maurice considers himself jokingly the "poor" relative. They may perhaps be described as the new hearth of Maurice's retiring years. The genial quality of these numerous luncheons has strengthened Maurice's long and deep friendships with Leonard Block and Joe Mailman; and it is this same setting which developed Maurice's friendship with Julian Bach, the editor of this book, and with Leon Hess, who gave birth to the idea of and generously funded this handsome autobiography.

These vignettes give some picture of the person behind the man. We urge the reader to look behind the extraordinary accomplishments of Maurice, and the sweep of the great historical events in which he was both witness and participant, for the many clues to the wonderfully caring and involved human being who lives behind the black and white print. We hope that, in doing so, you too, will share in some measure the richness of reward that we, who know, love and are loved by Maurice, so dearly treasure.

Marjory and Howard Cohen

November 1989
New York, New York

Preface

THE GENESIS of this book has, I believe, substantially some additional autobiographical interest and these several additional pages give me much satisfaction. Over the many years, I have met numerous communal leaders, in their own areas with very successful business or professional careers. Happily in quite a number of instances that professional contact developed into close friendships which conditioned my own life and in some cases changed the lives of the others. Indeed in one case the friend openly regretted that he had not met me earlier as it would have conditioned his own and his family's course.

Amongst the friends who admitted me to their personal lives - three are "way out" in front: Mr. and & Mrs. Felix M. Warburg, Mr. and Mrs. Henry Moses, and Mr. & Mrs. Leonard Block and their families.

Leonard and Adele are responsible for my friendship for and adoration of Mr. & Mrs. Leon Hess which has enriched a large portion of the last six or seven years of my days. Mr. Hess has hosted a small Round Table at the Harmonie Club on most Saturdays and Sundays, save the summer months, and at the height of the playing schedule of his Jets football team. Among his guests have been Joe Mailman, a communal leader, Eli Ellis, a well-known international lawyer and specialist in maritime affairs, Dr. Max Som, a leading ear, nose and throat specialist ripe with well-known honors, Leonard Block, Julian Bach, a leading author's agent or obstetrician, who has played an important part in the creation of this volume, and Jack Rudin, a communal leader.

Business problems were never discussed. The bulk of the discussions centered on local, political, and communal topics, worldwide situations including the Near and Middle East. When discussions dealt with the latter two areas, I may have contributed out of my residence there for some ten years, and my knowledge of the terrain, the political complexion of the leaders and, so, I added to the depth of the discussion. In

xi

all of these years, I do not recollect even one discussion of fund raising. I hope that I helped make some affairs alive and better understood.

Some three or four years ago, Mr. Hess began to urge me to do an autobiography which he would fund. I resisted because of my sculpture commitments, where I thought I still had something to say. Early in March 1989, Leon again referred to the book and mentioned his proposal to employ a writer to do most of the work on such a volume. I could no longer refuse to go along.

Over the years I had amassed much material, en passant, but not intended to portray my life. Here's the list of what I later turned over to Murray Teigh Bloom, one of the writers whom Julian Bach sent to me and from whom to choose:

Some one hundred typed pages of recollections of my earliest days while I was growing up, prepared solely for my family at their urging.

A mass of documents dealing with my affairs abroad for Mr. Felix Warburg, which I had given to the Hebrew Union College in Cincinnati for their historical collection.

"Living History" projects I had already compiled for the Ben-Gurion University in Beersheba; the American Jewish Committee; the Federation of Jewish Philanthropies of NYC; and the Council of Jewish Federations and Welfare Funds, which are all typed and aggregate hundreds of pages.

Sanford Solender's pages devoted to my life in *The Turbulent Years*, a two-volume story of the development communally of the American Jews — generously dedicated to me by my colleagues.

The introductions to each of the three volumes of my sculpture with much biographical data.

Additionally, after Mr. Bloom had steeped himself in the above, we had about twenty two-and-a-half hour personal conversations on certain areas which he wanted enlarged and placed in the proper time frames. Together we went over his draft line-by-line with my having the final decisions.

I'm sure, and so is everybody else, that this book will not become a best seller. I hope that those who read it or skim through it will feel rewarded and that Mr. Hess's determination to publish it gives him some inner satisfaction because he is such a modest man with so little to be modest about.

Maurice B. Hexter

Saranac Lake, New York
August 1989

Life
Size

Prologue

THE DEBATE over autobiography is still going on. Michel Montaigne, one of the great wise men, pointed to the basic problem: "There is no description equal in difficulty to a description of oneself." But that universal sage and very practical American, Benjamin Franklin saw another aspect: "The next best thing to living one's life over again seems to be a recollection of that life and to make that recollection as durable as possible by putting it down in writing." Some fifty-six years later Heinrich Heine, like myself a Jew, thought it was a foolish undertaking: "To write a criticism of one's self would be an impossible task. . . . I would be a fool to proclaim to the world the defects of which I am conscious."

Still, if it were to be done, good sense or no, what form should it take? Rousseau laid the law down firmly: "I have freely told the good and the bad, have hid nothing wicked, added nothing good." A more modern and much more modest writer, George Orwell, laid down the ultimate test for any autobiography: "Trust no autobiography unless it reveals something disgraceful about the writer."

Do I qualify under that most stringent test? As you will find later in this account, there was a time in my early life, doing some amateur, seat-of-the-pants casework, when I came up with a solution that would surely appall students in any of the three schools of social work I helped found. I can almost see their young, open mouths voicing a mixture of youthful incredulity and shock: "How could you?" The answer is, I did, I did. 'Twas a different age, another world practically — and it was the only way to save man's health, even his life.

1

On two occasions, in my mature middle years, I committed abroad what would now be deemed as criminal acts, felonies surely. But both times I operated with a clear conscience: I was saving endangered lives. And it was the custom of the country.

One of the advantages of autobiography is that it enables the writer to enjoy prophetic hindsight. For example, long before the expression was common I was on a "hit list" of terrorists. In 1932. More macabre — and menacing — they were Jewish terrorists. It wasn't much consolation that only days before I had narrowly escaped an ambush set by *Arab* terrorists.

There is also a retrospective feel-good aspect of autobiography. I was trusted by two of the most fascinating and shrewdest men of my time: Felix Warburg, a profound non-Zionist, and David Ben-Gurion, a prototypical Zionist. But then I was also trusted by a clever, greedy, and tyrannical despot, Trujillo. If there is indeed a balancing of accounts in the Ultimate Computer Records, Trujillo is surely entitled to at least one plus: He saved five thousand Jewish lives from certain death in Hitler's camps.

I was also thrust into the company of splendid monomaniacs who achieved their goals in spite of incredible odds. Their single-minded concentration on getting valuable chemicals out of the Dead Sea, on creating electric power for Palestine, on buying Arab land, made me feel like a dilettante juggling several different tasks. To make matters chancier, I was an outsider — a non-Zionist — in a world of true believers. I was saved often because they hated each other more than they did me.

The path to that singular destiny in Palestine was an odd, irregular one — one that could have only been plotted by playful, ironically amused fates. At nine, as a diligent, penny-pinching newsboy in Cincinnati, I didn't depend on Horatio Alger strategies like saving a rich man's child from a runaway horse. Rather, I catered often to hundreds of Cincinnati whores who generously gave the pint-sized newsboy five and even ten cents for the two-cent paper, delivered to their gaudy doors. As a result I later became a federal "expert"— at a munificent ten dollars a day — on the types and pricing arrangements of the city's hundreds of bordellos.

For all those raffish early intervals I was happily married for fifty-eight years, even as I was aware of the extramarital drives of a great man who helped shape my life and destiny: Felix Warburg. (But then, I never had the incredible charm he possessed.)

I acquired some questionable habits, along with millions of other American men. At eighteen I became both a bourbon drinker — two drinks a day — and a Lucky Strike smoker. The latter I remained until I was seventy-three, when I abandoned my three packs a day because some-one bet me one hundred dollars that I couldn't.

I had other qualities, sometimes not altogether admirable. When I was leaving a highly demanding job at Federation of Jewish Charities in New York a friend — a *friend*, mind you — said to the search committee, "What we need is a son-of-a-bitch like Maurice." He meant it, and in a way he was right.

At some point in everyone's life there comes a time when you fall into reverie about roads not taken, the might-have-beens, the fateful decisions to do A instead of B. There were at least two major turning points in my life where the road forked sharply, and I've often wondered what life would have been like if I had opted for the other road. The first was a decision in 1925, at Harvard, where I was an untenured member of the faculty, but one with promise. I could have stayed on in an academic ca-reer, which I would have loved: major investigations of mysterious busi-ness cycles? serious econometric discoveries? a future as a Presidential advisor on economics? Who knows?

The other fateful decision? In 1948 I was offered a cabinet post in Ben-Gurion's government in newly formed Israel, even though I was an Ameri-can citizen *and* a venerable non-Zionist. I could have had a major role in the making of a new land's history. . . .

Somewhere in *Faust*, Goethe observes that the ways in which deliberate design and pure luck are connected in the products of human action are something that few could understand. To this day I'm not sure that I do. But reveries have their own life force.

So here, reveries, warts, and all, is my story.

3

Maurice Hexter at the age of five in Cincinnati

1

Beginnings

ACCORDING to the ancient rhyme I was born "full of grace," as a Tuesday child. I was also a middle child, four years behind my brother, Leo, and three years ahead of Betty. Modern researchers conclude that a middle child manifests "greater dependency behavior"; seeks more adult help and approval than the first or later born; spends more time in individual activity; is generally more talkative. Middle children also tend to be more creative than firstborns. Of course no one knew this back then, which was probably just as well for me.

All this commenced on June 30, 1891 in a lower-middle-class section of Cincinnati. It was not a particularly vintage year for emerging but Averill Harriman also arrived that year, in far grander circumstances. Eighteen ninety-one was also the year Carnegie Hall opened and Herman Melville closed. And the first of the Sherlock Holmes stories started appearing in London.

My father, Max Hexter, was born in Hoechst, Germany, the site of a large chemical company. "Hexter" is surely derived from that name. My mother, Sarah Beck, came from a town near Dresden and was related to the famous Rabbi Baeck. My father had come to America when he was in his mid-twenties and had a little capital. I never found out how he came to invest most of it in an oil well in Ohio. The drilling ran out and the oil didn't. (Years later a Rockefeller company got the lease on the well and brought in a minor gusher by going down another two hundred feet.)

My parents met here through cousins, the Blocks. After marriage my father opened a little candy store near the old Cincinnati & Ohio railway station. But he clearly wasn't intended for retailing. For one thing, he was hard of hearing, with a middle-ear condition. Still, Cincinnati wasn't a bad place for promising beginnings. The Kroger chain started there; so did the Snyder Ketchup Company, which later became Campbell Soup.

We had a small apartment behind the store. We spoke German at home, as half of the city's families probably did. (As a result of my early German fluency, which I still have, I sometimes will favor a sentence structure with the verb at the end.)

At five I was enrolled in the nearby 5th District School,, which was next to Hughes High School. My first day at school was a shameful catastrophe and I had to be sent home: The newly imposed disciplines, the hostile environment, made me pee in my pants. Worse was to follow. It now appeared that I had inherited my father's hard-of-hearing condition. Genetics was barely a word then, let alone a science, but the connection was made. It became more certain when it turned out that my sister, Betty, was also afflicted. I wasn't a particularly dutiful student — I'm sure that my inability to hear well was a factor — and I encountered the disciplinary process often. Usually I would be banished to the clothing closet for a spell. Or merely receive a sharp rap on the knuckles with a long ruler.

Money was tight. At eight, I started selling newspapers — almost at the same time I started reading Horatio Alger stories of Dan the Newsboy, Pluck and Luck, and Paddle Your Own Canoe. I had two newsboy careers, morning and afternoon. It was quickly apparent that I was a morning person, and getting up at 4:45 wasn't a great hardship. I'd take the streetcar to a downtown printing plant that turned out a very special daily called the Court Index, a mini-version of dailies like the *New York Law Journal*. It provided the only information for lawyers on which courtrooms were to be used for what cases at what time. I had a key to the plant and I would find the corner where the big sheets of the index were placed. First I had to fold them down into smaller sheets. That was easy. The hard part was delivery of 135 copies to lawyers' offices, nearly all of them in fairly high office buildings: eighteen stories at the First National Bank Building, fourteen at the Atlas National Bank, a mere ten at the Union Trust. As a rule elevators weren't running that early in the morning. If I got lucky I'd find an elevator that was taking up the cleaning women, but mostly it was a lot of hiking up and down.

I was finished by 8:00 A.M. and walked to school by way of a Greek candy store, Marooden's, where I had breakfast of a kind — a chocolate sundae, for three cents. (I always asked them to put on lots of chocolate.) After a while I'd be greeted when I came in with a "Good morning, Lots." I'd get a flat $1.50 a week for delivery of the Court Index, minus fifteen cents

Life Size

carfare, or a net of $1.35 — it sounds impossibly minuscule today but you have to keep in mind that in those days a pound of round steak cost thirteen cents and a dozen eggs twenty-one cents. You could rent a fairly decent apartment for eighteen dollars a month.

After school let out, at 3:00 P.M., I'd go to the newspaper plants of the *Cincinnati Post* and the *Times–Star.* I'd pay half a cent per paper and sell them for two cents. But before I picked up the papers I'd stop at a little restaurant called Riggs Manhattan, started by a couple from New York. I'd have an order of hotcakes with maple syrup — and you could have all of the syrup you wanted. (Chocolate *and* maple syrup every weekday! No, I never had acne.)

Sundays meant getting to the *Cincinnati Inquirer* plant about 4:00 A.M. to get a bundle of the much thicker Sunday papers. These cost two cents and were supposed to sell for a nickel. Mostly I did residential deliveries right to the door, and every now and then I'd get a windfall: a quarter or even a fifty-cent piece from a big spender. I made at least two dollars on Sundays.

My father was an orthodox Jew who attended a conservative congregation. He walked to it on Saturdays, even though it was a very long walk. He recited his morning prayers, went to *schul* regularly, and I'm sure obeyed the 613 commandments. Naturally we had a kosher home. (To this day I can't eat pork.) My father saw to it that I was enrolled in the Saturday- and Sunday-school classes. On Saturdays I managed to get evicted in about twenty minutes by talking and I'd run to the public library to read far more interesting volumes, such as Mark Twain's. I probably was a premature agnostic.

When I was ten I made an interesting discovery. Ordinary people paid regular prices for daily newspapers, but there was a sizable element in the city that was far more generous to a newsboy who would come to them. At the turn of the century Cincinnati had a red light district with hundreds of bordellos. St. Louis and Cincinnati were the only two American cities that ever attempted to control prostitution by registering and inspecting the whores.

By selling papers in the district, usually for five or ten cents, I did much better. I also got to know the various houses and their pricing policies, an odd specialty that later led to a nice windfall.

Propinquity breeds attempt — or contempt, some cynic once said. I was physically eligible but much too frightened of the women I sold to. This was an age long, long before sex had become a commonplace for youngsters. (As for contempt: They were staunch loyal customers who always overpaid. Bless them.)

Beginnings

I was a young man with ferocious energy. What else did I do to earn money? The corn-silk connection. Farmers would come into town with fresh vegetables. During the corn season I'd go under their wagons and pick up the corn silk in the husks that had been pulled from the ears to show the customer what he was getting. There was a market for corn silk: The W.S. Merril Chemical Company paid five cents a pound. It was used somehow in their patented cough syrup.

I discovered basic business principles early. I could add to my earnings by buying the corn silk from other young gatherers for three cents a pound because they wanted to avoid the long trip to the chemical company. I usually made one dollar a day net — and I never tried to smoke corn silk. Much too valuable.

I was introspective and shy. Partial deafness didn't help, but I must have been persuasive. Every morning on the way to pick up papers I'd pass the Berry Bros. Varnish Company. In the window was a red express wagon available as a premium for buying varnish. By my fifth or sixth try I persuaded the owner to give me the little wagon, which became an enormous help in carrying my newspapers and the corn silk.

Things also improved at home. The candy store had long vanished and now my father managed to get a loan to buy an oil-delivery route and a horse-drawn tank wagon that carried oil and naphtha to residential customers, who used them for cooking and lighting. I often joined him. We'd go through the streets ringing our bell to announce our presence. We went into apartment houses, took the empty cans, filled them at the faucets of the truck, and then collected the money. It was a big day when my father collected six dollars, because that threw off a net of two dollars. We usually took sandwiches from home and stopped at a saloon to have a beer with the sandwich. Our favorite was a German "Zum Huenerhloch" (chicken's behind). Things got better and my parents were able to buy a house at 912 Richmond Street, a big step up. It cost three thousand dollars, a lot of money then. We lived on the first floor and had a tenant upstairs. We even had a phone installed when it was still a comparative rarity.

I had two good friends: Sidney, the boy who lived upstairs, and Rachel Manischewitz, who lived nearby. Ray's family baked matzos and were on their way to become a Jewish tradition. (As I write this the old firm was worth forty-five million dollars.) Sidney's family moved to Hamilton, Ohio, twenty miles from us and easily traveled on the interurban trolley. There was a large reservoir and Sidney and I chipped in to buy

Life Size

a used canoe. Once we canoed from Hamilton down the Miami River, a three-day trip, and then back. I picked up a tent and sometimes I would take the canoe up the Ohio River and set up my tent for the weekend. There was a Coney Island–like resort on the river to which steamboats would carry people to and from the city. To get to my primitive little camp I'd sometimes get on the stern of the boat at the wharf and ride up to where my tent was located, jump in the river, and swim for shore. It wasn't the only idiotic daring I displayed in those years.

I had an insatiable curiosity about places and people — particularly raffish ones — and one of the particular attractions was the Latonia racetrack, over the river in Kentucky. It was a sleazy, second-rate dirt track. Generally the Latonia Jockey Club was given a thirty-day running season in June.

I got a job as a hot walker, a stablehand who walks horses after an exercise run. When I was twelve I got promoted to jockey and rode in ten or twelve races, which paid me fifty dollars per. (The owner provided the silks and boots.) I was about five feet four inches and weighed 110 pounds, not ideal jockey statistics, but permissible. I think if I had ever won there would have been great embarrassment all around. Of course, I didn't know then that jockeys couldn't get life insurance. Racing was considered even riskier than steeple-jacking. I'm sure it wouldn't have mattered if I *had* known. Kids have no intimations of mortality.

Inevitably came time for my bar mitzvah. It called for intense make-up study, because I had not been a good student at the Saturday and Sunday Hebrew school sessions. With the concentrated study came an awareness of the religious community around me. I was fascinated by a neighboring family, the Isaacs, who were *really* orthodox. On Friday night they'd disconnect their telephone so it wouldn't ring on the Sabbath. One of the men in the family, a heavy cigar smoker, would smoke a lot on Friday and blow the smoke into test tubes, which he would cork. On Saturdays when he couldn't smoke he'd open the test tubes, one at a time, and inhale deeply.

Religion began playing an increasingly divisive role in our own family. My father decided that his first born, Leo, should become a rabbi, and should go to Hebrew Union College. Leo didn't last long there and dropped out. It led to a bitter time between my father and my brother and contributed, I'm sure, to Leo's lack of focus in his life. A terrible waste: I considered myself pretty bright, but Leo was far smarter. But he was in the wrong family at the wrong time. For many years he retreated into gambling and heavy drinking.

Beginnings

It was a particularly difficult time for him and my father because by then my parents had bought a larger house on Avondale. We occupied the whole house and in order to make the mortgage payments my mother took in boarders, mostly students at Hebrew Union College, which then had no dormitories. One of the students my mother took care of was Julius Mark, who later became Rabbi Mark of Temple Emanu-El in New York. The contrast between good student Julius Mark and my brother was too marked. For a time, Leo ran away.

I sold papers through most of my intermediate and some high-school years. I was a good student, somehow, and skipped at least two grades, in spite of playing hooky from time to time. Corporal punishment was still approved — when I got whacked by the principal, it was the last time I skipped school.

In Hughes High School I was introduced to anti-Semitism. The common cry was, "Hughes, Hughes, niggers and Jews." Cincinnati was just north of the Mason–Dixon Line and had been once a key stop on the underground railway for escaped slaves. But Blacks and Jews were a distinct minority in the school. I had become a prodigious reader and didn't mind in the least that there were no Jewish fraternities in high school.

Out of the blue came my great gift from Uncle Sam himself. Well, one of his minions: the Bureau of Immigration. The bureau was conducting a nationwide study on the importation of prostitutes into America — even though experts had told them there was more than enough local talent — and now the investigators had come to Cincinnati. The white slave trade was a very hot subject then. One of the investigators talked to a local newspaper editor, who thought a moment and recommended a young twelve-year-old hustling newsboy who knew the red light district better than anyone. A kid who sold more *Times–Star* papers to whores and their customers than anyone else. Me.

I managed to keep my mouth closed when they mentioned the "expert" fee they could pay me: ten dollars a day. (Twenty dollars a week was a good salary then.) For that I was to guide them through the district and give them the pricing level of each house: which were the $2, $3, the $5, and even the plush $10, the top of the line. There were hundreds of houses, so it could not be done in a day. The task took ten days, which gave me one hundred dollars and a minor mention somewhere in the voluminous report the immigration people finally did on the subject.

In my senior year we had talks about college. I hoped to get away from home to a private college in the Northeast, but my father said there just wasn't enough money. So college would have to be the University of Cin-

Life Size

cinnati, which was then the second city-run liberal arts college in the nation. (CCNY, now City College of the City University of New York, was
the first.) Tuition at Cincinnati was two hundred dollars a year and I'd
have to earn it.

There were jobs at school for willing students. My first was typing—
although I never learned the touch system—for a geology professor. I
transcribed his handwritten notes. The pay was better than selling newspapers and it didn't involve long trips and a lot of carrying.

Other opportunities emerged. I began teaching English three evenings
a week to some of the new immigrants at the Jewish Settlement House.
This was 1910, when I was a junior, and the great influx of East European Jews was reaching a peak. Another job, much less proper: One of our
rich local ladies, Helen Trounstein, was making a study of the dance halls.
She was certain that they were being used to induce girls to enter prostitution. There was a law that no one under eighteen could enter those halls,
but she was certain it wasn't being enforced. Thus my job: to find out how
old the girls were. To get to the dance halls I needed a car and she lent
me her Model-T Ford, which I learned to operate in an afternoon. At the
halls I had to dance with the girls and find out who was under eighteen
and where they lived. I then discovered two things about myself: I don't
like dancing and I don't like being a snitch. More than half the girls were
under eighteen and Helen Trounstein, a minor local power, managed to
get a lot of the dance halls closed.

In college I also began working for Professor Robert C. Brooks, a political scientist, who gave me research tasks. It was congenial work and
by my junior year I wondered out loud to Professor Brooks if, after all,
I might not think of a career of college teaching. He shook his head, sadly, and pointed out that as far as he knew there wasn't a single Jew teaching political science then at the college or university level anywhere in
the country. The odds were bad, he said. (The prevailing academic anti-
Semitism had a remarkably long run: it didn't die until after World War
II.)

There was a certain consistency of the policy. A couple of gentile
friends who were presidents of their fraternities apologized for not being able to propose me for membership.

As a sweetener for this disappointment Brooks came up with a possible consolation prize. The National Municipal League was meeting in
Cincinnati—then one of the most corrupt cities in the country—and from
the balance of the convention funds they announced a prize essay contest with a two hundred dollar first prize. Professor Brooks urged me to

Beginnings

try for it. I took three days off from school and banged out a longish piece on how American cities could obtain the reform so badly needed. A few months later my mother told me she had forgotten to give me a letter. I opened it and there was a congratulatory letter and a check for two hundred dollars. A marvelous sum for those days — a full year's tuition.

If I wasn't to go into college teaching there was only one other path: law school. Under local rules that prevailed at a lot of colleges until World War II you could spend your senior year as a first-year student in law school, if your grades were good enough. I elected that path and long before the year was out realized this was not for me. I had some adolescent moral qualms: If I won a case it meant someone had to lose, and so on. But in truth I simply felt uncomfortable in law study.

I graduated from college in 1912 — my one year in law school counted as my senior year — but I was not at the ceremony, because I had agreed to help my mentor, now my friend, Professor Robert Brooks, in two matters: He had taken a job with Swarthmore College and he was doing a study for the National Education Association on teachers' salaries. I was working on that.

In the fall I was the beneficiary of a nationwide reform movement that led to the creation of the Municipal Research Bureau. I did several jobs for them: on police personnel policies; on local traffic rerouting, which led to my being called "Expert Hexter" in the *Cincinnati Times*. But expert or no, I still didn't have a real *job*. Just then fate intervened forcefully and I was firmly set on a path that was to endure for many decades, with interesting detours here and there. The instrument of fate was Dr. Boris Bogen, a Russian immigrant who had managed to get a doctorate in education at the University of Moscow — which had far worse restrictions on Jewish students than we had here — and had come to America. Here he took up social service, which was just a notion then. So in January 1913, at the age of twenty-two, I entered the office of the United Jewish Charities of Cincinnati, which had been formed in 1896. (Boston had been the first, in 1895, to unite its Jewish charities.)

He had asked me to work for him, he later told me, because he liked the way I handled the evening English classes at the Settlement House when I was in college. "I liked the way you stayed put when the bell rang," he said. "You didn't rush out but remained to answer questions for ten or fifteen minutes." That, he added, made him think that I could be trained for social work.

In a way he constituted the first major Jewish social-work school. The pay was not great — fifty dollars for the first three months and then fifty

Life Size

dollars a month — but considering the tuition was free it was riches. And,
of course, I was living at home.

Dr. Bogen had a large family, with four boys and three girls and an interesting, well-educated wife. In time I became one of the family.

Beginnings

2

Apprenticeship

M Y FIRST two assignments clearly indicated that Jewish social work was never going to be a nine-to-five job. During the day I learned family casework by receiving applicants in the office, listening carefully to their problems and woes and visiting them at home to see if the facts jibed. Sometimes they didn't. In the evening I'd teach English at the Settlement House at 415 Clinton Street, patterned after the famous Hull House in Chicago, where I had taught English.

In addition the United Jewish Charities had a good-sized clinic directed by a fine internist, Dr. Daniel Heyn, and an inspired trained nurse, Mrs. Minnie Wiener, who actually taught me most of what I learned about family casework. There was also a foster home for children and a convalescent home for patients discharged from the Jewish hospital, which was not under the direct control of the United Jewish Charities; neither, at the time, was the Home for the Aged. We also had a clothing department based on hand-me-downs from friends — the sort of stuff now sent to thrift shops.

Every night except Friday, I was in charge of various clubs for children and teaching English to new arrivals. I was working about seventy hours a week but I was learning about a brand-new world. There was a small perk. Several times a week Dr. Bogen would take me out to lunch.

He urged me to spend any spare time looking over the old records of the organization. "You learn a lot that way," he assured me. One day I found record #1708 and a great surprise. It was about a loan of two hundred dollars to one Max Hexter, who had a wife, Sarah, a son, Leo, and an infant Hexter. It detailed how Max Hexter had lost most of his money in an oil-drilling venture but was hard working. It also recorded that the loan had been repaid.

leaders of the Cincinnati Jewish community was
Max Senior, who rightly should be called the father of modern Jewish
philanthropy. He gave me a graduate course in human relations and the
philosophy of giving *and* doing. He was the driving force in creating the
United Jewish Charities of Cincinnati and when he died, in 1939, he was
praised as "the chief guide of Jewish social work in America."

His family was descended from a long line of Sephardic notables, including the last crown rabbi of Castille. Max Senior had an older brother, Edward, who was the true business brain of the pair. They were part-
ners in distilling bourbon in Ohio and then in 1904 they entered a new
world: gunpowder. The Senior Powder Company became one of the most
successful of the independents, eventually challenging the "trust" headed
by DuPont, with the creation of a powerful group of independent powder makers. Edward Senior was interested only in business. But his younger brother, Max, had other ideas. In 1921, when he was fifty-nine, he retired, and really got into his stride as the benevolent genius of Cincinnati.
Up to then he had been devoting only half his time to various charities.
A wealthy bachelor without a family, he devoted all his time to improv-
ing the lot of the people of his city. He pioneered the city's park system;
helped create a clinic for the promotion of Negro health and welfare; spon-
sored the Model Homes Company, which carried out one of the first practical attempts at low-cost housing. He was also a major influence on an
entire generation of newcomers to Jewish communal service.

He kept a sharp eye on his beloved city. Once he called me in: "Did you
know there's a provision in the Ohio penal code that prevents the location of a saloon within three hundred yards of a public school? There are
a lot of saloons violating that law. I want you to go out and pinpoint the
saloons and the schools on this map." I did, and in time some thirty-one
saloons closed.

The learn-by-doing concept of Dr. Bogen was sometimes like a boot-
camp initiation. I came to the office one day at 9 o'clock and found a couple
with six children in the waiting room. I couldn't get any intelligible information out of them and suddenly the phone in Dr. Bogen's empty office
rang. I went to answer it and fielded several questions for a few minutes.
When I came out the couple was gone but their children, aged three to fourteen, were still there. The kids had no useful information, let alone a family
name or address, and I was up a tree. Fortunately, Dr. Bogen came in a
few minutes later and when he was filled in, he smiled and said a little grim-

Apprenticeship

ly: "We've got to flush them out. You'll see." What he did was phone two Yiddish newspaper editors in New York and Chicago, and give them the story. The punchline was that unless the parents showed up in three days we were turning over the children to a *Catholic* orphanage, since we didn't know that they were Jewish. Both papers ran the story and the next morning the parents showed up and took their children away. We had kept them for a few nights in our own House of Transients.

Why did a small Federation like ours need a transient home? We called our clients "traveling gentlemen" or "Wandering Jews"—with a certain amount of ironic inflection. They were recent immigrants, mostly men but a few women, who would go from city to city, presumably looking for work or for some distant relatives. They'd stay two weeks and, their welcome worn out, would be given train fare to another city, where presumably their work quest would be solved. Eventually the hot-potato simile became obvious and embarrassing all around. The National Conference on Jewish Charities appointed a Transient Committee to resolve disputes between city Federations where one of these travelers *really* lived.

There were other boggy areas you learned to traverse delicately. How do you handle the rivalries between the wealthy Jewish family dynasties — the Seniors, the Freibergs, and the Blochs? What one group gave to the others wouldn't. Which is why the home for the aged and the hospital were outside our Federation.

Max Senior once described the kind of giving games he had to play. "Back when we were getting the Federation on its feet here I went to a rich man, Simon Kuhn, a member of the family of Kuhn, Loeb. I knew the Kuhns were mortal enemies of the Freibergs, and when I went to see Mr. Kuhn about giving he said quite abruptly: 'Never mind, I'll give you twice what Maurice Freiberg will give you.' Well, that was a good start, so I called on Mr. Freiberg and he said he wouldn't give me a dime: he didn't like the federation concept. I said, you know Kuhn is giving me twice what you give me, and since you're giving me nothing . . . Freiberg's eyes gleamed: He said that? And he sat down and wrote out a big check, solely, I'm sure, because he figured that Kuhn would be discommoded by having to double the amount."

There were far rougher fund-raising devices in Cincinnati. There was a campaign among orthodox Jews in Cincinnati for the local Talmud Torah. There were two kosher butchers in the city, which then had about twenty-five thousand Jewish families. And both were cleaning up. One day the soliciting committee went to one of the butchers, a Mr. Osherowitz. They had a card for him and had been told not to accept any-

thing less than $5,000. (In today's terms, $100,000). The butcher exploded:
"You must be crazy! I'll give you one hundred dollars." They wouldn't take it. A day later the soliciting committee and a prominent local orthodox rabbi visited the butcher.

"I understand you offered only one hundred dollars," the rabbi said.

"Yes, rabbi," the butcher replied. "Believe me, it's a fantastic sum they're asking, but since you've come personally, I'll give five hundred dollars."

The rabbi shook his head. "No, Mr. Osherowitz, if you don't give five thousand dollars your meat will suddenly become *trayf*, this afternoon."

The butcher was rooted to the spot for a couple of minutes, but managed to get to his office in the back and write out a check for $5,000.

There were other fund-raising lessons to be learned: Jews must be asked only by Jews. A Jew never resents being asked for charity; he may bargain but he never resents your asking. Non-Jews are generous in their wills but Jews are more generous during their lifetime. The considerable disparity between giving in the here and now and the thereafter became a major debating point when some midwest Jewish communities were considering joining their local institutions in a city-wide Community Fund. Most didn't join.

Life was not all casework and fund raising. We had an interesting rich bachelor on our Federation Board, Sidney E. Pritz, who later became president. He was tall and handsome and pushed me to do a lot of reading in sociology and philosophy. He gave me books and the entire problem of philosophy and professional ethics came to a test when he invited me to be a chaperone at his elaborate camp on Big Tupper Lake, in the Adirondacks. That summer he was going to entertain a noted guest at his lodge: Alma Gluck. She had been born Reba Fiersohn in Rumania and brought to America as a child. She worked as a secretary, got married, and began taking singing lessons. In 1909 she was signed by the Metropolitan Opera in New York and stayed there four years. Later she concentrated on recordings and her beautiful soprano voice filled millions of Victrola discs. Her early marriage was dissolving. In 1914 she was divorced and she married the violinist Efrem Zimbalist. If I recall correctly, it must have been the summer of 1913 that she went to the Adirondacks to be a Pritz house guest.

The rules for a male chaperone were never spelled out so what I did, conscientiously, was look away. It was a very nice two-week vacation and gave me my first enthusiastic knowledge of the area. Curiously enough, in the biography of her mother, *Too Strong for Fantasy*, Alma Gluck's daughter, Marcia Davenport, doesn't mention Sidney Pritz, so perhaps

Apprenticeship

it was only a short-lived romance between marriages. (Sidney encouraged me to date his niece, a member of the wealthy Freiberg family, but it didn't gel.)

One of the great advantages of working for Dr. Bogen and the United Jewish Charities of Cincinnati was that it was the best place for recruiting trained social workers and administrators. I assumed my apprenticeship was over when in the spring of 1914 I was invited to come to Milwaukee to be interviewed for a job heading their local Federation. I was put up at the posh Plankinton Hotel and set out on a series of interviews. Even during the course of the talks I sensed that there were tensions between these Federation leaders. But by now I was accustomed to that.

When it was over I was offered the job at $150 a month, a great improvement over my Cincinnati pay; but now I'd have to provide for my room and meals and send money home to my parents.

There were some local roadblocks they expected me to remove. Morris Miller, the head of a large local knitting mill, was on the interviewing committee. He had a nephew, Nathan Goodman, who hadn't worked out in business and so he was eased into the job of head of their Family Service Agency. Nothing unusual. Social-service work then was seen as fit for business failures and general misfits. I may not have known everything about social work, but it became clear within a few weeks that young Hexter, aged twenty-three, knew a lot more than young Goodman. He resigned and I had complete control of the local Federation.

That was just a finger exercise. It soon became clear that the enmity between A.L. Saltzstein, the president of the Federation, and Charles Friend, president of the Family Service Agency, was firmly rooted and bitter. To complicate matters, Mr. Friend was distantly related to one of my mentors, Max Senior. I could see that I would have to traverse this terrain with great skill — and luck.

I had no illusions to start with. I knew I'd be the sole employee. A secretary? Ridiculous. The office was submiserable and I got permission to move to a slightly better location, a small one-story house with no basement. I had to heat the place with a stove. A new, rich friend, Max Freschl, vice-president of Holepruf Hosiery, called on me one day and exclaimed, "Hey, you're freezing here." The next day he arranged to have linoleum laid down to retain heat in the room better.

I was twenty-three and looked even younger, which presented problems. People would come in and say, "I have an appointment with Mr. Hexter," carefully looking past me. And I'd have to explain that I was *Mr.*

Life Size

Hexter. How could a young fellow like me solve their tough problems?

Within the first couple of months I won over the local powers because I remembered a useful bit of advice from Max Senior: "Always go through your current caseload carefully—somewhere in those records are relatives who can take care of their kin."

So I started going through the records carefully, and I was appalled. Record keeping was minimal and what little there was was chaotic. Then I got lucky. In going over the bare records of the eight people we had in a home for the aged I realized we had almost nothing about them, their families and backgrounds. I went out to talk to them and met a Mr. and Mrs. Singer, who were Hungarian and very pleasant. At one point they mentioned casually that they had a niece, had I heard of her, Edna Ferber? Of course I had. Most of America had. Edna Ferber had been born in Milwaukee and had worked on one of the local dailies before moving on. Her first novel, *Dawn O'Hara*, was a best-seller.

I wrote to her in New York telling her about her aunt and uncle in the home for the aged. There was no obligation, I said, but "I wonder if you might not care to undertake their support." She replied she hadn't known about the Singers but yes, they were her aunt and uncle. She enclosed a check for three hundred dollars and promised to send one hundred dollars a month thereafter for their support.

The Federation officers were delighted. From then on I was the embodiment of modern social work. Still, I had to keep in mind the advice Dr. Bogen had given me on how to get along with your boards. Rule one: Don't tell a board member he's wrong during an argument. Instead, say "I haven't made myself clear on this." That way you don't insult him and you plant a seed in his mind that when you do make yourself clear, he'll agree. Rule two: You must always be on *tap* but never on *top*. Rule three: Don't win your golf matches when playing with a board member.

For my first real venture away from home I had managed to find a pleasant friendly substitute. I had a room and breakfast at the home of a Mrs. Dannenbaum, who had two daughters. The community outdid itself in hospitality and several nights a week I'd be invited out—to still another chicken dinner.

There was a family who had done well in the shoe business. *Reich* had been transformed to *Rich*, but there wasn't much they could do about their three daughters, who were unattractive. The Women's Sewing Society met at the Rich home every Thursday and I would go there and have a cup of coffee and a slice of good cake, and meet the community.

On one visit I met the daughter of the president of the sewing society,

Apprenticeship

Mrs. Emanuel Philips. The daughter was back from Wellesley and we took to each other, dating frequently. Finally, very much in love, I proposed, was joyfully accepted. Mrs. Philips was delighted; Mr. P wasn't. From his viewpoint a son-in-law who made a mere $150 a month was bad enough. Much worse, there was no future in social work. We were still in love but those were the days when a heavy-handed father could detour the true course. We continued to date — Mrs. Philips felt that in time her husband would come around — but there was a pall on the romance. Eventually it simply drifted into nothingness.

I had been in the community only six months when my stock shot up sharply. Out of the blue I was asked to come to Montreal to be interviewed by the head of their local Federation, a prominent barrister. It massaged my ego to be asked and I went for an interview. He did offer me the job, at a considerably higher salary, but I wasn't yet ready to become an expatriate.

On my return to Milwaukee I was presented with one of the most unusual challenges I ever had in social work. A man named Pechonek, from Milwaukee, had been sent to a TB sanitarium in Wauwatosa. His symptoms vanished and he was discharged. He came home, had a bad relapse. Now he was sitting in front of me trying to tell me the truth, instead of some fudged concoction.

I pointed out that this was the second relapse he'd had after coming home. He nodded. "I got trouble at home," he said. What kind? "My wife. She needs it every night."

It took a few seconds before it dawned on me what he meant. "Every night?" Every night. They had several children, so divorce was obviously no solution here. Then I had an idea and I assured him I'd solve the problem but he had to do exactly what I ordered. Anything, he said.

First, we got them a larger apartment and the service picked up the extra rent. But in the second month we cut back on the money, which meant the family had to come up with more. How? The obvious solution — all around — was to take in a male boarder. Jewish, of course. It worked out. My client didn't have to return to the sanitarium and the family was held together.

Admittedly, in retrospect it sounds like a French-Jewish-farce premise. But there weren't too many real choices. There were no psychotherapists or social workers with clinical training, let alone sex therapists. And everybody knew that TB recovereds were particularly delicate. He was our client and we solved his immediate problem.

There were other difficult family problems, most of them stemming

Life Size

from recent immigration. The man usually came over first and worked very hard at two or three jobs, saving every penny so he could bring over his wife and children. Frequently, his arduous schedule led to illness and need for agency support. When the family came over there was a great gap between the newly Americanized male and the "greenies," his wife and children.

Two Milwaukee women contributed their own piecemeal solutions to the problem. One of them, Mrs. Kander, brought together and edited what was to become an enduring best-seller: *The Settlement Cook Book.* Another, Mrs. Sonya Rubin, began a series of classes for newly arrived immigrant women on how to dress American (including the then-essential corset). All this work stemmed out of the Abraham Lincoln House, the settlement center. Here Golda Meyerson got much of her assistance and start toward an extraordinary career that climaxed in her becoming prime minister of Israel.

Meanwhile I had become friendly with two sociology professors at the University of Wisconsin. This was many years before there were any schools of social work, and the sociology departments then handled what little training there was to be had. So for one summer session of six weeks I assisted Professor E. A. Ross. In the course of that period I became friends with Marguerite Mock, a student, who was elected to Phi Beta Kappa in her junior year. She was friendly with a faculty member, Professor Wolfenson, who taught, of all things, Patristic Greek and the Bible. I knew that he wanted to marry her. Still, I was invited several times to Madison and to dinner at Marguerite's dorm.

World War I had now been going on three years. My prime mentor, Dr. Bogen, was asked to take charge of the Joint Distribution Committee, which had been founded in 1914 to coordinate the overseas relief work of the American Jewish Relief Committee. Its first president was New York financier Felix Warburg, a legendary figure.

I was asked to come back to Cincinnati and succeed Dr. Bogen. It wasn't an easy decision: I had made a lot of friends in Milwaukee. But the offer was irresistible. I knew it would be a lot more difficult — Cincinnati had 27,000 Jews compared to Milwaukee's 9,000 — but I felt I had learned a great deal of how to handle the local "power structure" and that I was now ready to take on the volatile situation in Cincinnati. Also, my salary would be doubled — from $150 to $300. And I would be able to live at home.

What made the transition easier was that I had kept up with friends

Apprenticeship

in Cincinnati – with Max Senior, who was still very active; and with Sidney Pritz, still a romantic bachelor, who was now president of the Cincinnati Federation. A lot of Jews had made their fortunes in the bourbon business, but there were other avenues of success. The Pollaks were in the steel business and later merged with Inland Steel of Chicago. The Joseph family got rich through a fascinating form of ingenuity. As the war wore on there was a great shortage of dyes, because these had come from the German chemical industry. The Josephs sent out a crew of people to acquire all the dyed cotton thread they could, then put the thread through a process that sucked out the dyes used.

My father got involved in helping out the war effort in his own way. There was a great shortage of platinum, which the United States now needed. Someone told my father that dentists used platinum pins when they fixed false teeth into a patient's mouth. If you got an old set of teeth you got the platinum plug. So he went around buying the old false teeth. He would bring them home and boil them in a large kettle to get the platinum out. An ounce of platinum was then worth $180, so my father made some money. The rest of us suffered: the stench of the melting teeth was awful.

Late in 1917 my brother, who was four years older, was drafted. But the war was over before he was sent overseas. I was deferred because I was the key support of my family.

The work in Cincinnati had expanded greatly and I had to scout around for assistants. I gained one, Harry Viteles, and soon lost him to Dr. Bogen for work in Europe with the JDC. I also renewed friendships with a lot of younger members of wealthy families, because every social-work administrator has to look ahead at least one generation for the oncoming community leaders. Through Nathan Ransohoff, whose father, Joseph, was one of the nation's great surgeons, I met his cousin, Beatrice Block. Her family owned a large Winton car, which they let me use when we went out on a date.

Somehow I even found time to do my first published investigatory report. Called "The Newsboys of Cincinnati," it ran sixty-two closely printed pages and was published by the Helen S. Trounstein Foundation. Miss Trounstein – the lady for whom I had done a much more ad hoc investigation of the ages of young girls in our local dance halls – had on her death established a foundation "devoted to the investigation of social problems, particularly in our city."

My report was serious, very sobering. Yes, I had once been one of those newsboys, but it turned out I was damned lucky. I had somehow avoided all the pitfalls of delinquency, poor health, perversion, bad feet, undernourishment, neuroses, and poor education that we found in our survey of several hundred local newsboys. About a third of the boys were Jewish. Despite my stress that the papers had to take greater responsibility for the boys, the report got a fair amount of local newspaper attention — but my major recommendation came to nothing. I had suggested, right up front in my "Summary and Recommendations": "The crippled veterans from our armies in France and Italy should be given a monopoly of the newspaper selling business, and boys under sixteen should be eliminated entirely from such work."

In spite of the Dickensian miseries I had uncovered in the newsboy report this was a happy, challenging period. I was in charge and felt I could handle almost any situation, whether it involved the power structure or casework. My responsibilities had increased considerably. We had a fine hospital, a well-run home for the aged, a convalescent home, a good foster home that provided day and night care for children. And there was a growing Jewish settlement and community center. It was a model setup that other large Jewish communities around the country envied and emulated.

Early in 1919 I received a phone call from David Stoneman, Boston's park commissioner. He was visiting Cincinnati to inspect our park system and he wondered if we could have dinner and talk.

It turned out that Boston was about to lose its executive vice-president of the Jewish Federation, Morris D. Waldman. I had met him once when he came through Milwaukee while I was there. Stoneman and another communal worker, Chester Teller, were looking at the working of Jewish federations in various midwest cities. They spent three days appraising in Milwaukee and in that time I got to know a lot about Morris Waldman.

He was brought to the United States from Hungary when he was four. Later he lectured at Columbia, became an ordained rabbi, and for a couple of years directed the Galveston Movement, created to direct East European immigrants away from the East Coast. For nine years he was managing director of the United Hebrew Charities of New York and then had gone on to Boston. He had lost out on becoming director of the newly formed New York Federation of Jewish Philanthropies, due mainly to the strong influence of Felix Warburg, who favored Dr. Goldwasser, an assistant superintendent of schools in New York. So Waldman had accepted the Boston job, and now after several successful years there he was ready to leave and enter business in partnership with a prominent Bos-

Apprenticeship

ton philanthropist, Arnold Hartman, forming the Pacific Development Co.

Morris Waldman was only twelve years older than I was, but in terms of experience he was decades ahead. So I felt flattered that they considered me able to fill his shoes; that Morris Waldman had recommended me. I told Stoneman I had strong local ties and I liked what I was doing. Still, I would think it over carefully and phone him within two weeks.

It was a difficult decision. I talked to a few close friends, including Lillian Friend Marcus, who came from a leading New Orleans Jewish family. She felt that it would lead to wider development and deeper areas than Cincinnati ever would. There was another factor I didn't discuss with anyone. Boston also meant Harvard, and that meant the possibility of fulfilling an old dream: getting a doctorate from an Ivy League university.

In the spring of 1919 I took the train to Boston for interviews with Louis E. Kirstein, the head of Filene's, Judge A.K. Cohen, and David Ellis, chairman of the Public Service Commission. I met various other Jewish Boston notables and it seemed I passed muster. The position was officially offered to me — even after I had made it clear that I needed some time for myself working for a graduate degree at Harvard. They saw no problem in that. Shortly after my return to Cincinnati I phoned and told them that I accepted and would begin my work there on July 5, 1919.

Family

a photographic portfolio

Marguerite Mock Hexter in 1929.

25

Marguerite and Marjorie at six months, 1930.

The author with Marjorie and her nursemaid in St. Marks square, Venice, 1935.

Daughter Marjorie.

Marjorie's husband, Howard Cohen.

Granddaughter Teresa Abrams.

Step-grandson Dr. Jonathan Cohen.

Step-granddaughter Tamira Cohen.

Grandson John M. Abrams.

Cindi Abrams, granddaughter-in-law.

First great grandchild Kevin, 1985.

Marjorie holds grandson Kevin, flanked by his parents Dr. John Abrams and Cynthia.

29

Great grandson Kevin with aunts Terri and Tami.

The author with grandson John and great grandson Kevin at Saranac in 1989.

With John, Tami, Marjorie, Terri, and Howard Abrams, 1989.

With Kevin at Saranac, 1989.

30

3

Moving Up

IN PREPARATION for the Boston job I did a fair amount of reading about the Jewish community there. Even though Boston is one of the oldest cities in North America, it wasn't until the mid-nineteenth century that an organized Jewish community evolved. There had been individual Sephardic Jews around as early as 1649, when Solomon Franco proposed to settle there, but he was paid to leave the province. According to a 1674 tax list there were two Jews present and in 1720 a Jew, Isaac Lopez, was elected town constable.

Not until 1842 was the first congregation established, and it had great difficulty in trying to obtain cemetery land. By 1875 the best estimate was that there were 3,000 Jews in the area and they had established three congregations. By 1895 there were 20,000, of whom 14,000 were recent immigrants. When I arrived there were about 125,000 Jews in Boston. Nearly all of the communal organizations date from the latter half of the nineteenth century, with most of them established by German Jews. Later came parallel organizations set up by Russian Jews. By 1895 there were enough similar groups to warrant the creation of the Federation of Jewish Charities, one of the first of its kind in America. As elsewhere, there was a conflict in interests and even outlook between the older and generally richer German Jews and the more recent arrivals. I knew this would be a major problem — as it was in other large cities.

My living arrangements were temporarily solved by being put up in July at the Kernwood Country Club, near Salem, fifty minutes from the city by train.

When I got down to work I quickly discovered that I was the beneficiary of some great pioneering work Morris Waldman had done in Boston. His District Services Plan consisted of five separate districts in the city with separate offices. Instead of having to go to a variety of agencies in the different parts of the city you could get them all at a district office. Each district was run by a local committee as well as by representatives of the Federation. They met twice a month and did a fine job. Still, there were a lot of problem areas that I would have to work on.

One of the most important was a small hospital in Roxbury called Beth Israel, which had been opened by a group of orthodox Jews. It wasn't a very good hospital and I could foresee grave problems. The first job was to get a well-known community leader to take charge. I persuaded A. A. Ginsberg to take over and initiate a fund-raising campaign. As it happened, there was a great boom in Boston real estate from 1908 through 1919, and several fortunes were established. With that initial step accomplished I now had to find a major Jewish community leader to take on the presidency of the hospital. The obvious choice was one of the wisest and most respected Jewish leaders, Louis E. Kirstein, who after a retailing career had joined Filene's Department Store in 1912 as a vice-president and subsequently became a director of the Federated Department Stores. He was well-known locally, having served as president of the public library and as chairman of the Port Authority.

What I planned was to remove the hospital from Roxbury and build it anew in Brookline, next to Harvard Medical School. I felt that propinquity would surely raise the hospital's standards and help solve the problem of qualified Jewish students who were being denied admission to medical school. (One of the evasive reasons given was that medical schools in the area had no Jewish hospital where their students could get clinical training.) Once the plans for the new hospital were under way I was able to persuade Dr. Charles Wilensky to head it. He was a great administrator, had independent means, and had been head of the city's child-care program. And of course he knew exactly the right buttons to touch politically. In time the new Beth Israel emerged to become one of the nation's great teaching hospitals. It is one of my deepest prides.

From previous experience I knew that I would encounter some internecine battles among Federation leaders. In the Boston case it came down to a running battle between Abraham C. Ratshesky, who had been the previous president of the Federation, and Louis Kirstein. Ratshesky was a local Republican bigwig who founded the United States Trust Company in 1895. He was very genial, but a tightwad. He was also a tyrant, and altogether not a good man to have to work with. When he was replaced in 1919, after ten years as president, by Lou Kirstein it made my professional life much easier. Still, he was a power and liked to show muscle from time to time. Since he and Kirstein never got along there were inevitably fireworks.

We decided to publish an annual report for the Federation that would include the names of the givers and the amounts. Just as we were about to issue it I got a call from Mr. Ratshesky. He said he had just heard what was being done and he *ordered* me not to issue the report as I planned. I temporized, saying, "I've got to talk to Mr. Kirstein about it. He's my president." Ratshesky concluded ominously, "If he issues it there's going to be trouble."

I went to see Mr. Kirstein. He smiled broadly. "He said that, did he? Well, on the first fifty reports you mail, just put on special delivery stamps."

As far as I was concerned one of President Hoover's notable accomplishments was appointing banker Ratshesky United States ambassador to Czechoslovakia in 1930. At least it got him out of Boston — and the Federation — for a few years. At the time he was appointed the local gag was, "He got the job because he can tell a bad check from a good Czech."

When I arrived in Boston in July I could hardly wait to set in motion my own private ambition — registration at Harvard's graduate school. In September I entered the Department of Social Ethics. I had to arrange my courses either for early morning or early lunchtime. My office then was only twenty minutes by subway to Harvard Square. Most of my work was done with Professor Richard Cabot and James Ford. It was Cabot who suggested my first published work under academic auspices. He pointed out that there was a great need for case studies to teach social work in a manner similar to Harvard Law School's approach. He was so persuasive that I agreed, even though it meant a nearly impossible schedule for me. Fortunately, I was able to get Sol Drucker, who was then head of the Federation orphanage, to collaborate and in 1924 the book finally emerged as *Children Astray*, published by the Harvard University Press. It was the first case book on social work ever published, and it sold out completely.

In 1920, a year after my arrival in Boston, I had a great honor thrust on me: I was elected president of the Conference of Jewish Charities, which represented federations or similar amalgamations in seventy-five cities around the country. The 1921 annual meeting of the conference took place in Milwaukee.

Several weeks before the conference I got an invitation from my friend

Moving Up

34   Marguerite Mock to have dinner at her home. We had kept in touch spo-
radically. I knew that she was now teaching in the Milwaukee public
schools, that her father's livery business was going downhill fast, that
she had long ago refused her professional friend's offer of marriage. I also
knew that her uncle, a prominent trial lawyer in Wisconsin, had told her
it would be a mistake to marry a social worker. Only men who couldn't
do anything else would drift into such a field, he felt. It was a fairly typical
attitude of the time, probably exacerbated by the fact that the Mock family had come to America in the 1840s: an old-line-families-know-best kind
of snobbism, I suppose. But there was a genuine attraction between us,
which was why we had kept in touch.

    Instead of dinner together we arranged a picnic at Donges Bay on the
north shore of the lake. It was a good time to take a fuller, more serious
measure of one another. She was twenty-four and we had known each
other on and off for five years. The next day we became engaged, but
not before I laid out honestly the problems she'd have to face in Boston
as Mrs. Maurice Hexter. Part of the considerable burden would inevitably fall on her: I would be putting in eighty-hour weeks; I would probably be out five or six evenings a week on Federation business; I still had
to send part of my salary home to support my parents. I was making a
splendid eight thousand dollars a year, very good for the time; but there
would not be much family time together.

    We were married on August 11, 1921, and took a lake trip from Chica-
go to Buffalo, visiting Niagara Falls along with thousands of other newly married couples that summer. We took a train to Pittsfield, Massachusetts, where I had left my new car, a lovely twelve-cylinder National
Roadster, and drove through New England leisurely for an ideal honeymoon. Then I brought my bride to my temporary bachelor home at the
Kernwood Country Club, of which I was now secretary. (In return I paid
no rental or club fees.)

    In the fall we looked around for permanent quarters and chose one
of the Federation community centers in the south end. Then after a year
to another community center in the west end. Later on we had our own
apartment on Commonwealth Avenue.

    The year 1921 was a curious one in some ways. Fate has a way of hint-
ing at the future. Fortunately most of us can't read those hints of things
to come. The event was a kind of showdown, in Boston, of two opposed
forces existing then in world Zionism. Chaim Weizmann, the eminent
British chemist who was the leader of the world Zionists, had come to
the States with Albert Einstein, already celebrated as one of the most origi-

Life Size

nal thinkers in physics, who was a Nobel Prize winner *and* a confirmed Zionist. He and Weizmann formed a powerful team. Their ostensible object was to raise American money for the cause, but also to win out ideologically over an American group headed by Supreme Court Justice Louis D. Brandeis and Rabbi Stephen Wise. The Brandeis group had the concept of building Palestine through private investments. The Weizmann idea was that what was needed was "national money" that had to be soaked into the ground, so to speak, to build up an infrastructure. It was money that a central body would spend to build roads, drain swamps, retrain European city dwellers to be farmers — things that couldn't be done by private initiative that called for repayment and even profit.

In the end the Weizmann group won out and their opponents retired formally from American Zionism to form the Palestine Economic Corporation to help set up industry and business in that land. I followed the arguments of the debate with some interest. I was impressed by Weizmann's arguments, and by his enormous charm; but nowhere was there any readable hint that before too long I would be intimately, even dangerously, involved in that continuing debate.

In my carefully scheduled time for academic work I had firmly decided that my doctoral thesis would deal with Jewish communal organization to provide insights into a subject which no one had tackled before. I had always been attracted by the study of statistical methods — what a fine bunch of statistical tables I had formulated in my newsboy study! — and I took a course given by Professor Edmund Ezra Day (later president of Cornell University). It was a great course and Day asked me to help him on a text on statistical methodology.

This was a time when economic data were getting newer and more sophisticated looks, partly as a result of work being done by Warren Persons at the very new Harvard Business School. Persons was revolutionizing the way economists were looking at economic data at a time when there was growing interest in the business of cycles. He had isolated various trends: the secular, the long-term, and seasonal variation. From these he evolved variations in the cycles. I found the results particularly interesting and took my tables — done laboriously by hand in that primitive age before electric calculating machines, let alone computers — to Professor Young. He went through it and asked: "Ah, is this going to be your thesis?" I said, no, I was going to work in the field of Jewish communal services. "A mistake. Make this your thesis. You've got something novel here. Anyone can write history. This is real, *useful* research." It was a jolt. At least a careful study of Jewish communal services would have been related

Moving Up

to my day-and-night line of work and would have been an additional and impressive credential in the community. This new theme was just about totally unrelated, and worse, highly technical.

What I had done was analyze the way Professor Persons had looked at business statistics. I broke down birth, divorce, and death rates and found that they were surprisingly cyclical and — even better — that they had predictive value. In short, if one of these series went down before another one you could predict three or four months in advance how the other series would react. In a way it was one of several valuable contributions made by other economists that led to our present series of "leading indicators," the ones that the government now publishes regularly. They are "leading" not in the sense that they're the most important but that they have *predictive* value. They will tell you in advance, with a considerable degree of accuracy, what's going to happen. But you have to select and test those leading indicators with great care. The fact that the number of storks in Holland this year exactly matches the number of births next year doesn't mean one will always be a good predictor of the other.

Every doctoral student has to undergo a refined inquisition known as "the Orals." I was quizzed by six or seven professors representing the departments in which I had taken courses. Each of the tenured men, specialists in some comparatively narrow ambit, was out to trip you up. That was inevitable, but they were even more interested in how you handled your answers. How ready were you to say, "I'm not sure," or even, "I don't know?" It is a grueling time, some of which is spent inwardly berating yourself for not having done reading on this or that arcane and narrow specialty. At the end of five hours, just when you're drained mentally and physically, you're asked to step outside the room of torture, a room that seemed so comfortable and comforting when you entered.

You step outside for a few minutes, reviewing in exaggerated detail every mistake you made, every omission, every misplaced emphasis. The whole process surely must be an element in the makeup of Hell.

After what seemed like the passage of hours — it was only five minutes — the chairman came out and congratulated Doctor Hexter. Marguerite met me outside with the car, and a quart of ice cream. We celebrated with a good dinner. My endless night study was at an end.

A week earlier I had encountered another, less important part of the testing process: I had to pass the reading-knowledge requirement of two foreign languages, French and German. You could select any professor on your list to test you. I chose Professor Cabot, the head of the Department of Social Ethics, from which I had wandered far afield.

So I arranged to be tested by him in his Emerson Hall office. He asked which I wanted to take first. German, I said. That I knew *very* well. It was the French I was worried about. Cabot pulled down a German book and asked me to translate a paragraph. At one point I translated the word *dass* as *that*.

He interrupted. "No, *dass* means *the*.

I said, "Forgive me, but if it's *the* the word should have only one S, not two."

"By God, you're right," Cabot exclaimed. "You know more German than I do." Exam ended. Congratulations. I received my doctorate in 1924.

There is an old insult that students of statistics have to contend with: "There are three kinds of lies: lies, damned lies and statistics." While I was still working on my doctoral thesis I got involved in a minor skirmish in the world of statistics that had great significance to the Jewish community.

During the First World War the army had tested a great many inductees and subsequently published its findings. This led to a much-publicized book by the author of the tests which indicated that the inductees who came from eastern and southeastern Europe just didn't measure up to the other uneducated groups native to America. In short, the foreigners were stupider, had much lower IQs.

I went over the book and discussed it with a new friend, Dr. Abraham Meyerson, a pioneering American psychiatrist. It wasn't that we thought that Jews were naturally smarter or any similar nonsense. What fascinated us was that we saw how the psychologist had misused the statistics. We collaborated and did a long piece for *Mental Hygiene*: "A Study in Probable Error." It produced considerable reverberations and got a lot of publicity. It even came to the attention of Professor Frank W. Taussig, an eminent Harvard economist who was thought to be Jewish but worked hard to hide it. One day in the Harvard Yard he stopped me and smiled. "Hexter, I'm glad you did that article. It was getting too much even for me." (Actually I am being a bit unfair to Taussig. He was only half Jewish. His father, an emigrant from Prague, made a great American success story by becoming head of a major railroad. Professor Taussig's mother was a Protestant schoolteacher.)

I had been appointed an instructor in the Department of Economics. I also taught summers at the new School for Social Work at Simmons College. Meanwhile Marguerite had also decided, with my encouragement, to go back to teaching in the Boston public schools. This was an

Moving Up

age when wives didn't work at all. Every red-blooded American male felt it would be a stain on his honor — and his bread-winning abilities — if his wife had to work. But in our case there were two other factors: Marguerite was a marvelous teacher, equipped with incredible patience; and second, in an age when there were no pension systems in social service we felt it would be wise for her to keep her credentials as a teacher in order, in case anything happened to me. We wanted to have children but so far we hadn't had any luck.

The offending, and wildly inaccurate, book on the East European immigrants also served a not-so-subtle ideological argument for a bill Congress was considering, the National Origins Act, which was passed in 1924. It provided a severe quota system for immigration that favored northern European countries and cut catastrophically the immigrants allowed from Poland, Russia, Hungary, and Rumania. The bill was signed into law on May 26 by President Calvin Coolidge. It had been lobbied against by all major Jewish organizations. (The quota system had been voted in 1921, but the 1924 act was far more severe.)

Where were immigrants from those depressed countries, riddled with organized anti-Semitism, to go? Early in 1924 an unlikely haven seemed to emerge: Mexico.

Why Mexico, of all places? First, there was the story that the president of Mexico, Plutarco Calles, was half Jewish: His father, the story went, was a Jew from southern Turkey. Moreover, Calles was coming to Washington to get a large loan for his largely dormant country. As a kind of quid pro quo, he'd offer to open Mexico wide to Jewish immigration from Europe.

It sounded like good news to most Jews, but not to the ardent Zionists, who naturally felt that the place Jewish immigrants should head for was Palestine, not Mexico. Still, the big question remained: Even if Mexico *wanted* the immigrants, how likely an area was it for *mass* immigration? Nobody was thinking of a modest few hundreds or even thousands, but hundreds of thousands.

At this point the Emergency Committee on Jewish Refugees, which represented some thirty-three Jewish organizations ranging from the Amalgamated Clothing Workers Union to B'nai B'rith to the Zionist Organization of America — just about all of organized American Jewry — decided that a thorough investigation of Mexico's possibilities as a haven was needed. I was approached: Would I make the survey for them? It would take three months or so, they estimated. It seemed like a real challenge and Marguerite and I agreed that I ought to do it. The direc-

Life Size

tors of the Boston Federation agreed to give me leave — after all, this was a serious possibility for finding a home for a lot of imperiled European Jews — and in April 1924 I went to Washington to study governmental files and printed reports on Mexico. I talked to State Department people who had spent years in Mexico, and read many books on that country.

Another man, from Philadelphia, had been detailed by the committee to join me in the survey, but he proved a total goof-off. He's best left unnamed.

By the time I arrived in Aguascalientes by train from El Paso I knew certain basics. Jews had been in Mexico from the time of the Spanish Conquest. More than a century before Jews came to the Dutch colony of New Amsterdam in America, there were a number of Jews already in Mexico.

The Inquisition was established in Mexico in 1571 and the first auto-da-fe's flames crackled in 1574. At least several dozen men and women were burned at the stake in the next few years. Most of them were Marranos, Jews who had ostensibly converted to Catholicism. The powers of the Inquisition lasted right into the nineteenth century. But by 1825 to 1835 Jews from Germany began arriving in Mexico and were allowed to settle. There was no vestige of Jewish communal life until 1885, when the first synagogue was built. But there was no *real* Jewish communal life until 1922, two years before my arrival. After the first real immigration quotas were established by the United States, East European Jews started drifting into Vera Cruz. Most of them were Russian or Polish, Yiddish speaking, who had been peasants, minor entrepreneurs, or teachers escaping pogroms and officially sanctioned persecution. They would have preferred the United States, but weren't allowed in. Prior to World War I there were about seventy-five Jewish families living in Mexico City, most of them from Austria, Germany, and Alsace-Lorraine. A few dozen Jewish families were scattered throughout the rest of the country.

In Aguascalientes, I had a letter of introduction to the United States consul. I duly went to the Consulate and handed over my letter to the clerk, who shook his head, sadly. "I'm sorry, the consul died yesterday." Then he asked suddenly: "Where are you staying?" I mentioned the only hotel in town. The clerk grew pale: "My God, that's where he died of typhus." A dismal beginning, but I should add that in all my three months in Mexico I never got sick. Not even a touch of the inevitable *turista* stomach. (Of course I drank only bottled water and avoided fresh vegetables unless they were cooked thoroughly.)

I went to Guadalajara, the second-largest city in Mexico. I got myself settled and went out to the market place to seek out Jewish peddlers. How

Moving Up

did I know they were Jewish? Their lighter skins and taller physiques made me pretty sure. The final test: I spoke to them in Yiddish, and they responded. They had all kinds of terrible stories, usually involving hegiras that began in Poland. One man had crossed Russia and Siberia at the tail end of the revolutionary period. He worked his way to China and then again to San Francisco — where he was refused entry. He didn't have a quota number.

So he drifted down to Mexico and became one of the peddlers, an *ambulant*, literally someone who walks around. Even that entry level into business wasn't easy. You had to have a license to peddle and the local man who dispensed them was a Catholic priest. My much-traveled peddler went to the priest, who asked: "What is your religion?" and the peddler thought, My God is this the Inquisition all over again? Reluctantly, he admitted he was Jewish. The priest broke into a broad smile and shook his hand warmly. "Don't worry," he said. "I'm a Marrano." He gave the peddler a license.

It was a marvelous story — a priest descended from Jews forcibly converted God knows how many generations ago — and I went to visit him. He was quite cordial and proudly showed me the unusually large library he had of Hebrew books.

Some of the peddlers disclosed that rifts among Jews weren't confined to communal affairs in the States. The more recent arrivals were generally Yiddish speaking and they resented the advantage the prior Jewish immigrants had because they spoke Ladino, the Spanish dialect of the Sephardic Jews. Among the more settled Jews, who had established a YMHA, a YWHA, and a fairly large B'nai B'rith center in Mexico City, there was a continuing debate — not always on a polite level — between the assimilationists and the Zionists.

What made these sharp differences especially tragic was that in Mexico anti-Semitism was a constant factor. As one expert Jewish observer, Rabbi Martin Zielonka, put it: "The hand of the Inquisition still hangs heavy over Mexico. A resident observer, a wealthy Mexico City merchant told me: 'You have to be aware that the environment is strictly Latin and thoroughly Roman Catholic. There is a lack of tolerance, as known in Anglo-Saxon countries, and the danger exists that some political organization will avail itself of any animosity against the Jews, to find sufficient support for its political struggle.'"

After weeks of travel and interviews with Jewish leaders and many Mexican officials I had to conclude that there was no way that Mexico could absorb large numbers of Jewish immigrants. There were no large

Life Size

parcels of fertile soil that could be worked without large and expensive irrigation projects. As far as the urban situation was concerned it was clear that there wasn't any need for more peddlers; and there wasn't any large industry as a potential employer. In short, Mexico didn't have a middle class, stability, or an infrastructure that could readily absorb large numbers of immigrants.

I started writing my largely negative report in a small hotel near Chapultepec Park. (The era of Mexico City's luxury hotels was more than a quarter-century away.) What was surprising was that the cost of living in the city was very high, practically like New York. There was one small personal outcome: I learned to drink tequila

How prophetic were my recommendations? During and after World War II Mexico accepted very few Jewish refugees, and by 1950 a fair number had left the country for Israel. That year it was estimated that Mexico had around 27,000 Jews. Today it has about 35,000. As one native Jewish author put it recently: "Jewish instinctual fear of assimilation as well as their distrust of Mexicans has caused them to live in neighborhoods that remind one of medieval ghettos. Today in Mexico City, supermarkets, Jewish kindergartens and private schools are located in the Jewish ghettos of Tecamachalco or Polanco." Oh, yes — President Plutarco Calles never got the loan he wanted from the United States.

In 1914 the Joint Distribution Committee was formed to coordinate the overseas relief work of the American Jewish Relief Committee (German Jews), the Central Relief Committee (orthodox), and the People's Relief Committee (Jewish labor). Its first president was Felix Warburg, who made the JDC an effective relief agency in Eastern Europe right after World War I.

All communal officials, like myself, got involved in raising funds for the JDC, in addition to our own campaigns. Since Zionist fund raising was also a constant there was a strong move afoot to unite the efforts into a single United Jewish Campaign. It wasn't easy. The Zionists naturally resented money being sent to European relief that they felt would do more good building Palestine. On the other side were bitter anti-Zionists like Julius Rosenwald, the head of Sears Roebuck and a very generous JDC contributor: "I shall not lift a finger to advance the immigration of Jews to Palestine."

In its first decade (1916–26) the JDC raised some $60 million, of which $7 million went to Palestine. The Zionists on their own had sent $20 million to Palestine in the same period. Considerable sums now — for the

Moving Up

time, *enormous* sums.

The trouble then, as it often is now, was the USSR. There had been a disastrous series of crop failures, starting in 1921. Massive starvation led to thousands of Jews leaving the land for cities and jobs. In the beginning the JDC depended largely on the famous Herbert Hoover relief group, but soon it became clear that short-term solutions wouldn't be enough. Massive resettlements of Jews would be needed. The JDC thought it had an ideal area: the Crimea. In 1924 it created a new agency, the American Jewish Joint Agricultural Corporation, or Agro-Joint, to make the idea work. Julius Rosenwald, a confirmed anti-Zionist, gave $5 million and eventually about 200,000 Jews were colonizing more than three million good farmland acres in the Crimea. (This was still in the relatively benevolent time of Lenin's New Economic Policy, when Russians were allowed to farm their own land and conduct small businesses.) In the summer of 1926 I was asked to join a committee of four to go to Europe for the JDC to look at their activities and report. The JDC had started inviting executives of local federations to make such study trips, so there was nothing novel about this one except that one of our group was to be William Rosenwald, son of the Chicago philanthropist.

With me on the committee was an old friend and colleague, Jacob Billikopf. "Billi" was eight years older than I, and far more experienced. For a time my career seemed to tailgate his: He had, for example, preceded me in Cincinnati as head of the Jewish settlement, then in Milwaukee as head of the local Federation. He married Louis Marshall's daughter, and thus became a member of one of the nation's most prominent Jewish families.

Marshall, who had been born in Syracuse, N.Y., in 1856, had become a partner in Guggenheimer, Untermyer and Marshall, New York's leading Jewish law firm. He also was a founder of the American Jewish Committee and had served as its active president from 1912 to 1929. In short, he had become the chief spokesman of the German-Jewish elite in America. And he had also been a cofounder of the JDC.

A great natural leader and commanding speaker, Marshall spent a lot of his time defending Jewish civil rights in the United States and abroad. He had been patently unhappy when his daughter Ruth married Jacob Billikopf, who was not only an emigrant from the wrong side of the Jewish tracks — Vilna, in Poland — but was also a member of a still unaccepted profession, social work. In time, though, Marshall got over that unhappiness when he found that his new son-in-law was a great organizer and fund raiser, even if he wasn't a German Jew. Billi directed a campaign that raised $25 million for Jewish war relief during World War I. In 1919 Billi became executive director of the Philadelphia Federation of Jewish Charities, which was now his base.

Looking back on that first trip of East European discovery, several incidents remain engraved in memory. Yet I also marvel at our inability to pierce the veil of things to come, the murderous dark night of Stalinism and the gulag world.

Our first stop was in Lodz, a Polish textile center and major Jewish population center that was just beginning to recover from the ravages of World War I. Warsaw was in better shape. We then drove from Vilna, Kovno, and Bialystock to Riga, where I had my first sight of the midnight sun, that great marvel that enables you to see the sun set in the west and in a few moments rise in the east.

When we reached Riga, around 9:00 P.M., we were starved, because there just weren't any tourist facilities en route. In the hotel dining room I saw the Russian word *IKRA*, which I knew meant *caviar*. I translated the price into dollars and it turned out that a bowl cost only $1.20. It was great stuff and I greedily finished the bowl. When the bill came, I found, as most of us do at one time or another in life, that a little knowledge is indeed a dangerous thing. Yes, the price was $1.20 — *per gram*, or 1/28th of an ounce. My delicious caviar cost $18 or, in today's terms, around $100. I've had ambivalent feelings about caviar ever since.

We took a long, thirty-six-hour train trip to Moscow, where we met Dr. Joseph Rosen, who was in charge of the Agro-Joint project that fostered the Russian-Jewish colonization in the Crimea. There I became, very briefly, a nudist. The Bolsheviks had taken over the palatial homes of the old Russian aristocracy and made them into convalescent and rest homes for workers. It was a warm day and seemed like good swimming weather. I took a look at the beach and found everyone naked. When in Rome . . . . So I went in naked, and never felt so conspicuous in all my life.

The Ukraine had been put through a deliberate famine by Stalin to wipe out the independent peasants. The millions of rotting bodies throughout the Ukraine created a dangerous hazard. When we were driving south from Moscow you would know an hour before that you were approaching a large city from the overpowering smell of decaying bodies the officials hadn't been able to bury. The bodies were piled up under heaps of lime to lessen the nauseating intensity.

We knew Russia was becoming a severe police state. I suspect that one of the reasons I was selected for the trip was that at Harvard one of my

Moving Up

graduate students was a Pole named Dzerzinsky. His uncle was head of the dreaded OGPU, or secret police, until his recent elevation to his new post as chairman of the Supreme Economic Council. My student gave me a letter to his uncle and when I was in Moscow I visited Dzerzinsky, who was expecting me. "My nephew told me you were very helpful to him at Harvard and I want you to have this special pass. You will find it useful in your travels in my country."

It was. Once we were caught in a long line for a ferry at a point on the Dnieper River near where the Soviets had built their great new dam. Judging from the length of the line and from the capacity of the primitive ferry — pulled by hand ropes — we would have to wait all day. I took the Dzerzinsky pass to the guard at the head of the line. He did a double take at the official stationery, the Dzerzinsky signature, and promptly waved us right through to the head of the line.

Then there was a Russian-Jewish doctor who had been imprisoned because his *son* turned him in as a counter revolutionary. Dr.Rosen knew and needed the doctor and wondered if there was anything we could do to get him out of prison. We went to the local jail and showed the pass, and in less than an hour the doctor was released.

In many ways Joseph Rosen and the Agro-Joint had performed a minor miracle in getting 150,000 impoverished city Jews out onto the land and teaching them the basics of farming. A lot of them did pretty well for a while — until Stalin showed the real face of brutal totalitarianism. (I suspect that at least a few of the Soviet emigrés in Brighton Beach are descendents of those hardy Agro-Joint farming pioneers of the twenties.)

The caviar episode notwithstanding, the trip wasn't any kind of tourist joy. For most of the time we lived mainly on black bread and tomatoes, because there was no meat or chicken. At that we were eating better than nine out of ten Russians.

From Sevastapol we took the train to Moscow, which meant two nights of travel in a rundown sleeper, which, then as now, calls for mixing of the sexes in the same compartment, regardless of relationship. I had an upper berth and a former Russian aristocrat the lower.

After the first night the porter removed my bed sheets and when I asked why, told me he would return them the next night. My compartment companion, who spoke some German, saw my concern about getting the same sheets — none too clean to begin with — she lent me a set of her own sheets, which were completely fresh. (Five weeks later when I met my wife, as planned, in Vienna, I told her I had spent two nights with a Russian baroness and one night in her linens. Fortunately, by this time Marguerite

Life Size

had become used to my humorous imagination.)

After returning to Moscow, Dr. Rosen arranged for me to take an official plane to Danzig — my first flight, in an open two-seater. From Danzig I flew to Berlin on Lufthansa, and from Berlin to Bratislava, from where I proceeded by car to sub-Carpathia, in Czechoslovakia, which bordered on Rumania. The area surely should have qualified as the poorhouse of Europe. The JDC discovered a large group of impoverished Jews who had been isolated for decades. Our sleeping accommodations were generally with cows in the barn. JDC was helping the hand-to-mouth Jewish peasants greatly, but in traveling through the area you felt as if you had stepped back into the eighteenth century. The conditions we saw — and lived with — made all the poor Jews I had known in Cincinnati, Milwaukee, and Boston seem like comfortable middle-class citizens by comparison.

Our trip ended in Vienna, where Marguerite met me. She had been motoring in a new and very large Belgian Minerva car with a friend and her daughter. By slow stages we drove to Rotterdam, where we shipped the car to London. After London we did the grand tour of the British Isles. But even this enjoyable interlude failed to get rid of the collected impressions of the devastation, utter poverty, and famine we had witnessed.

When we returned to Boston I visited several cities under JDC auspices to tell what I had seen on my trip and how the JDC was helping our fellow Jews in Eastern Europe. The meetings helped raise money for the JDC. If I was effective in depicting the poverty and devastation that the JDC was trying to ameliorate, my tales doubtless invoked in a lot of my middle-class Jewish listeners the same inward prayer I had: Thank God my parents came to America when they did. Now, in 1926, it had become an almost impossible dream for just about all the Jews in those stricken areas of East Europe.

Moving Up

4

Toward Palestine

N
O SOONER was I back on the job in Boston than I was again caught up in not-so-silent battles taking place in every large Jewish community among Zionists, non-Zionists, and anti-Zionists. All above and beyond purely local battles of Big Giver A against Big Giver B; or the orthodox community against the reform. To make matters more intensely fratricidal, the local Zionists were still bitter about all the JDC money going to the Jewish farm colonies in Russia. Imagine all the good that money could have done to settle a lot of those farmers in Palestine instead of in communist Russia! they cried.

Louis Marshall, who was mildly sympathetic to Palestine even though officially a non-Zionist, urged Chaim Weizmann to come to America to help make peace between the warring factions. Weizmann arrived toward the end of 1926 and for the next several months traveled across the country trying to get his zealous Zionists to tone down their attacks on non-Zionists. He also worked very hard to get some influential fence sitters to meet him at least halfway. One of the men on whom he concentrated his incredible persuasive powers was Felix Warburg, an extraordinarily wealthy banker who was the first president of the JDC and probably, at the time, the best-known Jew in America.

During the first visit to America, as far back as 1922, Weizmann had paid particular attention to Frieda Warburg, Felix's wife. Weizmann had great charm, charisma, and an almost hypnotic eye. (He was, Winston Churchill once put it, a marvelous cross between Jesus Christ and Lenin.) Weizmann thoroughly charmed Mrs. Warburg and she in turn persuaded her husband to take an interest in that great international and histori-

cal project, Palestine. Once he was persuaded, Warburg, in turn, was able   47
to influence Louis Marshall. That got the ball rolling toward the major
agreement in March 1927 between the determined Zionists and the
reasonable non-Zionists such as Warburg, Marshall, and several other
key leaders of American Jewry. Weizmann and his old opponent, Justice
Louis Brandeis, had come up with an interesting compromise: A commission of experts should be sent to Palestine to survey its needs and decide what were the most efficient ways that money raised in different
funds could be used. So the Survey Committee was born. It was officially endorsed by a conference in New York at the Hotel Biltmore on March
22, 1927. As Louis Marshall put it: "The time has come when we should
forget everything but the fact that this problem of Palestine is a *Jewish*
problem."

The Survey Commission was to be nonpartisan. It would be directed
by an impressive group of prominent Jews of three countries: the United
States, Great Britain, and Germany. The directors were Louis Marshall
and Felix Warburg, non-Zionists; Lord Melchett (formerly Sir Alfred
Mond of Imperial Chemical Industries), a Zionist; Oscar Wasserman,
president of the Deutsche Bank of Berlin; and Dr. Lee K. Frankel, a vice-
president of the Metropolitan Life Insurance Company.

To celebrate this major decision a dinner was arranged at the Biltmore.
As it happened, I had gone to New York that morning on some Boston
Federation business. There was a popular train, the Merchants Limited,
that left Grand Central at 5:00 P.M.. As I was hurrying to catch that train
I met Louis Kirstein, president of the Boston Federation.

"Where are you going, Maurice?" he asked. I said I was catching the
five o'clock train back to Boston. He shook his head. "I have a better idea:
Weizmann and Marshall have just made peace today and there's a dinner in honor of that pact. I'm going. Come along and we'll take the midnight sleeper back." So with that chance meeting and the wise decision
of an employee to go along with his boss's wishes, a new course for my
life was created. I sat with Kirstein at his table near the dais. We had just
gotten to the appetizer when Lee Frankel came to our table and smiled
at me. "Maurice, you just saved me a phone call to Boston. I've just been
made chairman of the Joint Palestine Survey Committee and I'd like you
to be my secretary."

To many of us in those early days of Jewish social work Lee Frankel
was our wise father and friendly guide. Born in Philadelphia in 1867, he
was twenty-four years older than I. He was a brilliant student, became
a chemistry professor at the University of Pennsylvania, and was much

Toward Palestine

sought after as an industry consultant. A local rabbi helped arouse Frankel's interest in Jewish communal affairs and social work.

I never cease to marvel at the deceptively innocent — and seemingly minor — coincidences that govern the way our destinies are determined. Frankel was friendly with another Jewish chemistry professor, Morris Loeb of Columbia University. More to the point, Morris Loeb was a member of the preeminent Kuhn-Loeb family of New York. When the city's Jewish communal leaders were looking for someone to head the United Jewish Charities, Morris Loeb thought of his colleague in chemistry, Lee K. Frankel.

Frankel was one of the handsomest Jews I have ever met. He was tall and florid faced with premature white hair and a commanding presence. Not only was he presidential looking, he was an extraordinary organizer and doer as well. You don't get that combination too often.

After a few years running and building United Hebrew Charities — he was also responsible for the introduction of professional standards into Jewish philanthropy — he got interested in the new area of social insurance as a key to the prevention and relief of poverty. The obvious place to study it was the pioneer, Germany, where it has been legislated by Bismarck. The Russell Sage Foundation offered Frankel a sizable grant to go to Germany to study the plan's workings and write a report. His 1910 book, *Workmen's Insurance in Europe*, became a landmark work.

Shortly after it came out he was on the train going to Philadelphia to see his family. Next to him in the smoking car was a friendly man. They lit their cigars and started talking. "What do you do?" the stranger asked, and Frankel told him about his book, which had just been published. The genial stranger asked several penetrating questions, and soon Frankel realized this wasn't just parlor-car chat or idle curiosity. Indeed not. The stranger was the president of Metropolitan Life Insurance and vitally interested in the concept of social insurance. He could see that, properly applied, it could save his company millions of dollars every year.

Metropolitan Life, like many other insurance companies, was actively selling what they called "industrial policies"— in effect, the working man's life insurance. The small premiums were payable weekly and a company collector would come around and record the payment. If the insured died the company would pay his family the thousand dollars or so for which he was insured. (All this, of course, was decades before Social Security.)

The insurance executive did some quick inner calculations. If he could prolong the lives of only half of his industrial policyholders by a year —

just a year — the company would receive fifty-two more weekly payments per person to lend out for good interest rates. And it would have gained a year before it had to pay to the insureds' families.

So he persuaded Lee K. Frankel to leave United Jewish Charities and become a vice-president of Metropolitan Life, an unusual breakthrough for a Jew in those days. Frankel's earliest job with Metropolitan was to create the Visiting Nurses Association to visit sick patients who had an industrial policy. Just as the prescient president had foreseen, many lives were extended, many breadwinner policyholders lived longer, and the company did even better. With that success in hand Frankel became a power at the insurance company.

All this explains why a request by Lee K. Frankel was not turned down lightly by any of us in Jewish communal work. As it happened my boss, Louis Kirstein, didn't need any persuading. When I told Frankel I'd need Kirstein's okay, Frankel smiled — nothing easier — and in thirty seconds flat had Kirstein's approval to my taking temporary leave from the Boston federation.

I was asked to select two public health experts to take along with our party of experts. I chose Dr. Milton Rosenau, head of the Department of Preventive Medicine at Harvard School of Public Health, and Dr. Charles F. Wilensky, director of the newly reconstituted Beth Israel Hospital. Together with Lee Frankel and our respective wives we steamed to London, where we had meetings with several key Zionists such as Lord Melchett and Simon Marks of Marks & Spencer. From them we got a fairly clear picture of the Zionist operations.

In those days before air travel was common a long trip to Palestine was indeed an undertaking, generally punctuated by tourism. From London to Paris, which was in a holiday mood because a young American, Charles Lindbergh, had just arrived unconventionally — by air from New York. In Marseilles we met a Briton who was to become a familiar part of my life for many years: Colonel Hermann Frederick Kisch, D.S.O. and Croix de Guerre.

Kisch would have been a casting director's first choice for the typical English officer of the period: stiff, unapproachable, tall, lean, sporting a military moustache. He had come to Zionism through a totally improbable sequence of events that started with the Kisch family of Prague in the eighteen century. One branch of the family came to Britain early in the nineteenth century and in 1873 Hermann Michael Kisch, the colonel's father, entered the Indian civil service and rose to become director of the Indian post office. He returned to England in 1904 and became active in

Toward Palestine

Jewish affairs. Both his sons followed their father into government service. (The older brother, Cecil, became an authority on central banks.)

Colonel Kisch was born in Darjeeling, India in 1888, educated at Clifton College, which was for the Jewish elite of England their own version of Eton and Harrow. From there he went to the Royal Military Academy, Britain's West Point, where he ranked second in his class. Commissioned in the Royal Engineers, he returned to India. When World War I broke out he was shipped to France with the India Corps. He was wounded three times. Later he served in Mesopotamia, where he received another wound, which threatened him with total blindness. He was retired from active service and much decorated. He entered the Military Intelligence Directorate and acted as a British delegate to the Versailles Peace Conference. In 1922, while still in Paris, he got a telegram from Chaim Weizmann asking him to represent the Zionist movement in Palestine. He had already met Weizmann and was sympathetic to Palestine.

Kisch was a perfect choice for the task. He could talk to British officials of the Palestine Mandate as an equal, and he was a battle-hardened officer the Arabs would respect. He accepted the job, resigned his army commission, and moved to Palestine to become, as he put it, "the Jewish ambassador to the Palestine government."

The American party and Colonel Kisch steamed from Marseilles to Port Said and from there motored to Cairo. It was the end of June 1927 and in that ancient time, before air-conditioning, Cairo in the summer was a reasonable facsimile of Hell. It was too much for us effete northerners; we had to move from Cairo to Mena House near the Pyramids.

During our two days in Cairo we met with the heads of two leading Cairene Jewish families, the Cicurels and the Menasces. The Cicurels owned Cairo's leading department store and one of their daughters married a rising young French politician, Pierre Mendès-France, later to become France's prime minister. Baron Menasce, fabulously wealthy, had the world's outstanding jade collection, plus a serious Rolls Royce collection. These rich Sephardic Jews had the best of worlds: Egyptian citizens, they also enjoyed French citizenship, which meant they couldn't be tried in Egyptian courts; only French courts. They were generous and very friendly and entertained us royally.

They weren't Zionists, but were vaguely sympathetic. In those days the active Zionists were largely confined to Eastern Europe and, to a lesser extent, Germany and the United States.

From Cairo we drove on to Kantara, where we crossed the Suez Canal on a small ferry and then entrained on a night sleeper for Jerusalem.

Life Size

I was greatly moved when we first saw the Holy City's spires and cupolas. We put up at what was then the best — and the only — hotel in town, the Faust. By any other standards it would have been rated terrible.

We were awakened at 5:00 A.M. by a congress of braying donkeys outside our windows. Thorough and efficient, Colonel Kisch had mapped out itineraries for all of us: The public health hospital experts were to visit the existing institutions and the rest of us were to see the country from Dan to Beer Sheba as a whole; to see what the World Zionist Organization had been able to accomplish in the past twenty-five years.

It wasn't the best of times for a visit. A depression was under way, with much unemployment, which meant that the Zionist Organization was responding to a lot of unexpected calls for relief funds. On our visit to Haifa we encountered a large demonstration of the unemployed, who may have had some notion that we were bringing relief money with us. Another depressant: In 1927 the number of Jews leaving Palestine (5,000) exceeded those arriving (3,000).

At the British high commissioner's office we were briefed by Lord Plumer's aide, who summed up the role of Britain, the mandatory power, in his own fashion: "The job is to keep the Jews and Arabs from throwing stones at the Government at the same time." (By extension, throwing stones at each other, or even unilaterally at the government, was tolerable.) He related a recent visit of an Arab delegation who said that if the high commissioner persisted in a certain program they would not be responsible for what happened. Lord Plumer responded in true colonial fashion: "I haven't asked you to be responsible for what happens."

Inevitably we got briefings on the running debates between the Jews and the Arabs over the land's future. On the surface, the Arabs suddenly seemed like firm democrats. They wanted home rule, with a one-man, one-vote premise. The Jews, being in the minority, opposed it. There were all kinds of ingenious suggestions for how to guarantee the Jewish minority inviolable basic rights, but the Arabs insisted on simon-pure Western democracy. It did make some of us a little uncomfortable but we understood the real fears of the minority. Part of the problem was that among Semites — Jew and Arab alike — the word "compromise" did not have a favorite-word status. Things to Semites apparently are never gray: They're black or white. (Of course all statements about broad racial or ethnic characteristics are suspect, but deep down I still believe this one fairly valid.)

The obdurate Arab opposition to Jewish development in Palestine reminded me of the old story of the Sybilline books. Socrates once re-

Toward Palestine

ferred to the prophetess Sybil as "one of those inspired persons who has given many an intimation of the future which has saved them from falling." One day, the story goes, an Asiatic monarch went to Sybil. He said he was very much impressed by her predictions of the success of his reign and realm. He said he would like to buy her library of prophetic books. She said fine, he could have half of them for 10,000 gold ounces. "I wouldn't give you half of that for all of them." Six months later, after some of her newer prophecies had proven valid, he came back and offered to take up her original offer. No, she said, the price is now 20,000 gold ounces for one fourth of the books. He departed in fury. A few months later he came back and now her price was 20,000 for an eighth of the books. In short, with passing time the price always went up. I suspect that this applies to the Arabs and the Jews: They could have gotten a much better deal at the start of the bargaining than later.

We traveled through the country and realized just how barren it had been before the Zionists. Large stretches of the countryside were still desolate. The commonest kind of road was a dirt track and there were far more horse-drawn wagons than trucks or cars. In many settlements the dwellings were, at best, primitive. Arthur Koestler, who had come to a communal settlement in Hepzibah in 1926, after leaving the University of Vienna, recorded in one of his autobiographical volumes his shock at the settlement's "ramshackle dwellings in which only the poorest in Europe would live as an alternative to the discarded railways carriage."

(Koestler left another mark on Palestine. In 1928, as a columnist on the Revisionist daily *Doar Hayom* (Daily Post), he invented the Hebrew crossword puzzle, a specially difficult feat because the Hebrew alphabet consists of consonants only.)

One of the fabled figures I wanted to meet was Joshua Hankin, who had been the purchasing agent for the Zionists in acquiring land parcels from the Arabs — mostly wealthy absentee landowner Arab families who lived in Beirut. Hankin went from the Ukraine to Palestine in 1882. He quickly became friendly with Arab *fellaheen* and landowners and acquired fluent Arabic. When I first met Hankin I thought he looked like Christ or one of the biblical patriarchs. During his life he purchased more than 150,000 acres for the Jewish National Fund.

Another fascinating figure was Dr. Judah Magnes, who was married to a sister of Mrs. Louis Marshall. Dr. Magnes, who had been an American rabbi, came to Palestine to become head of what was to become the Hebrew University. Even then he was already a dissident from the prevailing Zionist viewpoint. He felt that greater efforts must be made to include the Arabs in a nondenominational Palestinian state.

There was a reunion with an old colleague: Harry Viteles, who had been one of the staff members back in Cincinnati. He left me to join the JDC and then had been sent to Palestine to take charge of the Central Bank of Cooperatives, which the JDC had funded.

I was impressed by the caliber of all the key figures I encountered that summer in Palestine. Yes, for the most part they were dreamers, but they also had a high can-do quotient. Theodore Herzl's much-quoted comment was appropriate here: "This is the secret which I hide from everyone: I am at the head of only boys and beggars . . . with dreams." Now they were converting dreams into promising realities.

In time the experts submitted their reports, which had to be put together in a combined report, to be supervised by me. We came back to Boston and my Federation duties, and teaching, and now I had the additional task of supervising and editing the combined report. The agreement had been that the Frankel Commission report would be completed within a year and now, in May of 1928, we were to meet in England at Lord Melchett's grand home, not far from the New Forest and Southampton, to go over the final draft.

The group that gathered there included Felix Warburg, Lee K. Frankel, Oscar Wasserman, myself, and of course Lord Melchett. His father, Ludwig Mond, had been a German chemist who had patented several processes involving sulphur, ammonia, and nickel. His younger son, Alfred Moritz Mond, our host, entered the family business and greatly expanded it until it became the giant Imperial Chemical Industries (ICI) in 1926. Mond entered Parliament in 1906 as a Liberal and later entered the cabinet of Lloyd George.

He had not been brought up as a Jew, but in his public life was often the butt of anti-Semitic slurs. This probably helped Chaim Weizmann win him over to Zionism in 1921, a truly remarkable conversion, since Mond had married a Christian and his children were confirmed and married as Christians. His friends were largely Christian, and he knew almost nothing of Judaism. Despite all of this, Mond became head of the English Zionist Federation and then chairman of the Council of Jewish Agency. He was blunt, direct, and sometimes rather blustering, but he had a great sense of humor. He collected caricatures of himself.

Melchett Court was a very proper large English country home with butler, valets, many maids, and enormous breakfast buffets. After breakfast we'd sit down to hack away at the final version of the Frankel Report. The only trouble was that Lee Frankel had suddenly taken serious-

Toward Palestine

ly ill in London. He had had a history of vertigo attacks but this time it was more serious: He had Ménière's disease, auditory vertigo, which is usually accompanied by deafness, nausea, and vomiting. As secretary to the chairman, I was appointed to replace him in preparing the final report.

During our stay at Melchett Court I got to know more about Mond's children. His son, who had married a niece of South African leader Jan Smuts, had absolutely no interest in Judaism, let alone the report we were working on. Yet, in time, he and his mother were both converted to the Zionist cause. She became president of the British section of the World Jewish Congress and he succeeded his father as chairman of the Council of the Jewish Agency. One of Lord Melchett's daughters, Eva, had married Lord Reading's son, a barrister. Another daughter was very much a social butterfly and led what the Victorians used to call, primly, "an irregular life." (Seeing Lord Melchett in London with this very sophisticated daughter, a local wit once gained fame with his wisecrack: "There's Mond and demi-Mond.")

We worked on the report and finally, with some minor changes, it was adopted. In effect, we put together the findings of our experts and came up with a draft report and conclusions. It was about two and a half inches thick and some six hundred pages long, and taught me an important if unoriginal lesson. Much earlier the British Royal Society, which is made up of experts in various scientific areas, had adopted a self-mocking Latin motto: "Nullius addictus jurare in verba magistri." Or in plain English: "Don't put your faith in the words of experts."

In retrospect it's easy to see where the experts went wrong. When you start with your first faulty assumption — in this case, water resources — everything that follows is going to be equally wrong. If you start out dubious about getting enough water for irrigation obviously you can't recommend increasing the farming population very much. Then other mistaken assumptions follow. It was a mess — and none of us dared assume we knew more than the experts did.

Our report did speak glowingly of Palestine's potential. We knew it wouldn't truly satisfy everybody, that the Zionists would be outraged that the idea of Palestine as a Jewish homeland did not receive a passing reference. Instead, Palestine was "the land of our origin." Like all documents that try to satisfy widely disparate parties, the report had to resort to euphemisms and occasional vagueness.

Still, if there was to be a Jewish Agency composed of Zionists and non-Zionists, a compromise of sorts was needed. What was involved was an agency with a council of 220 members evenly divided between the two blocs. Of the 110 non-Zionist seats, America — which was expected to supply a lot of money for the rebuilding of Palestine — was to receive at least 44. Within the Zionist groups there was bitter opposition to letting *any* non-Zionists serve on the agency. Vladimir Jabotinsky, the leader of the hard-line Zionist Revisionists, was firmly opposed. He thought the non-Zionists would emasculate the Zionist ideology. As more than one Zionist, including Ben-Gurion, put it: "Who needs all those *mishegoyim* with us?"

When we returned to Boston, in addition to my regular federation work and teaching at Harvard I had to select the American non-Zionists for the meeting in Zurich in the summer of 1929 that would ratify the mixed Jewish Agency. In our innocence most of us at the Melchett Court meetings hadn't realized the devilish difficulty in trying to define a "non-Zionist." Obviously it couldn't be an *anti*-Zionist; no Rosenwalds for this agency. What we finally arrived at was a catchall definition: anyone interested in and devoted to the development of Palestine. How did that differ from proper Zionists? Well, a non-Zionist had never enrolled in the Zionist movement and hadn't paid the *shekel*, the symbolic ancient coin (more modernly translated into "at least a dollar") in order to vote in Zionist matters. Not elegant, but serviceable.

It took Weizmann's great persuasive efforts to get the definition — and the accompanying fifty-fifty division of Jewish Agency members — accepted by the Zionists.

Underlying the distinction were some considerable ideological differences. Louis Marshall, a typical American non-Zionist, saw in Palestine two things: a place of refuge and a place where the Jewish spirit might thrive. The non-Zionists had little interest in statehood. In fact, they were *opposed* to statehood for Palestine. The key non-Zionists were firmly and well established in their own countries — the United States, Britain, and Germany — and had no desire to raise the disturbing spectrum of divided loyalties that a Jewish state might generate.

A British historian described the great divide this way: "Between the two parties was the extreme difference between those who are absolutely convinced of the absolute truth of an ideal and those who merely admire the ideal; between love and platonic friendship."

While we were still on the boat to Europe we had a wireless from Weizmann saying he was having great difficulty in getting the Zionists to go along on the fifty-fifty split on the Jewish Agency makeup. Our response, by return wire: It's fifty-fifty or we go home. We got to Paris late in the afternoon and at the request of Warburg and Marshall I was sent on ahead to Zurich and Weizmann. He said he was getting a lot of resistance from his diehards, who felt the equal split would dilute their influence; that they were selling out for the money which the non-Zionists were expected to produce. Weizmann seemed impressed by the firmness of the non-Zionist contingent and promised to redouble his efforts. He then did a lot of arm twisting via telephone and a few hours later called me to say the fifty-fifty principle was safe. Only then did I phone Paris to say it was all right to go to Zurich and the conference. It was an extraordinary affair in many ways: Not only were the world's great Jewish leaders there but there was also an impressive sprinkling of celebrities such as Albert Einstein, novelist Sholem Asch, and French politician Leon Blum.

In the summer of 1929, in Zurich's town hall, where the Zionist Congress was meeting, Chaim Weizmann finally triumphed over his right wing, the Revisionists. The Congress voted overwhelmingly to endorse the new pact on the Jewish Agency — the "pact of glory." After the vote Louis Marshall got a standing ovation, a touching tribute to a non-Zionist who had devoted a life to working for the welfare, and the rights, of the world's Jews. Now he would share the direction of a new group, the Jewish Agency, that would rebuild Palestine.

For many of the non-Zionists in attendance it was a fine time to get to know one another. A Briton, Sir Osmond d'Avigdor-Goldsmid, chaired the meeting. Ben-Zvi, later to become president of Israel, criticized the absence of the democratic process in the selection of the non-Zionist delegates. Sir Osmond took a long, look down his nose at this illogical Palestinian. After all, how could the non-Zionists organize their countries' non-Zionists to vote on this? But his answer to Ben-Zvi was more to the point: "Mr. Ben-Zvi, when I chair a meeting and decide that I have done a good job, I have no hesitancy in reappointing myself, and that is the democracy of Jewish community life where I come from."

The following morning, an unusual delegate got on the elevator of the Baur-au-lac Hotel in Zurich. He was Dr. Emanuel Libman of New York, one of the world's great diagnosticians. He was *the* consulting physician at Mt. Sinai in New York, whose personal patients included Albert Einstein, Chaim Weizmann, Sarah Bernhardt, and Lord Northcliffe. He had been active in the establishment of the Hebrew University and its medical school. A floor below, Louis Marshall and I got in the elevator. Dr. Libman gave Marshall a warm hello and a quick glance. When we reached the lobby Libman pulled me aside. "I'm afraid I have very bad news for

Life Size

you," he said.

"What is it?" I asked.

"Louis Marshall will be dead in within forty-eight hours."

From almost anyone else in the world such as firm mortal prophecy would have been greeted with incredulity. But Dr. Libman's reputation — some called him "an advance man for the *malech-ha-movis*" (angel of death) — preceded him. Once in the United States he attended a dinner at which President Harding was a guest. After a fast glimpse of the president, Dr. Libman told a friend that Harding would die within six months. He did.

It was a panicky moment. It was not the kind of "news" you could pass on. I promptly phoned a prominent local physician and asked if he would be available on short notice for the next day or two. It was a matter of life or death, I told him. He agreed. After breakfast, an hour after Dr. Libman had made his dread prohecy, Louis Marshall fell ill and returned to his room, where he grew worse and had to be removed to a hospital. There, on September 11, 1929, he died from complications following an emergency operation. In days before antibiotics *complications* was a common obituary term.

(The curious tricks memory plays on us. Today, sixty years after Louis Marshall's death, what I remember most vividly about him is a ridiculous bit of comic trivia. One night in Paris in 1927 I took him and Lee K. Frankel to the Folies Bergère with its semiclad show girls, an obligatory visit for every American visitor. Afterward I asked Marshall how he liked it. His grinning reply was a marvelous double pun: "I never saw so much navel engagement without the loss of semen.")

Even the grave illness of Louis Marshall couldn't put a damper on another ideological sideline battle. This concerned the nature of the Hebrew University. Here the struggle was between Judah Magnes and Chaim Weizmann. Ostensibly the issue was whether the Hebrew University should be governed on the American or European plan, under which the rector is the absolute boss — but the real issue was a struggle between Magnes and Weizmann.

Magnes, from San Francisco, was a reform rabbi, once at Temple Emanuel in New York, who had become head of the old Zionist Federation in 1905. He was also a pacifist and opposed the United States entry into World War I, which undermined his leadership in the Jewish community. In 1922 he and his family emigrated to Palestine, where three years later he became chancellor of the very new Hebrew University.

Magnes's conflict with Weizmann stemmed from his belief that Palestine should be a binational state of Arabs and Jews. He firmly did not believe in Jewish statehood, and Weizmann did. That issue wasn't resolved there, of course, but at least I did manage to get a temporary solution to the Hebrew University issue. The Board of Governors adopted my suggestion that a committee be formed to study the situation in Palestine to determine which form of governance was best for it.

Finally our business in Zurich was finished and a friend, Joseph C. Hyman, head of the JDC, and I headed for Paris and home. We had reservations on the *Ile de France* but when we checked out of our hotel in the morning the concierge told us to unpack — the ship wasn't sailing. She had hit the pier hard when docking and needed repairs. This was the season when all Americans headed home, so berths were scarce. Finally we managed to squeeze in a couple of berths on a smaller ship going from Liverpool to Montreal.

Back in Boston personal and professional problems awaited. First was the great news that my wife was pregnant, but the disturbing, unspoken footnote was that she had had two previous miscarriages. Second, I had to discuss with her a major career change that was looming, one in which she would be vitally concerned: I had been nominated in Zurich as one of two non-Zionist Americans for the Jewish Agency Executive, which meant residence in Jerusalem. The other, Maurice Karpf, had already indicated he was not prepared to live in Palestine, but would operate out of New York.

We had long talks at home.

I explained some factors that had made me accept Felix Warburg's offer. She already knew that I had reached a burn-out point on fund raising for Federation, that I was tired of mediating the continuing local battles among my big givers.

Clearly it was wiser, medically, that Marguerite stay behind temporarily, simply because the medical facilities in America were much better than Palestine's. We were *sure* that this time a normal birth would take place, and the idea of raising a child in Palestine was daunting. Obviously life wouldn't be nearly as comfortable for us in Jerusalem as it was in Boston. Not only would it be another world but also another language. Friends and family would be vastly distant. (There weren't any international phone lines from Palestine to the United States then, and surface mail took at least three weeks each way. Air mail was years away.) Marguerite wasn't nearly as enthusiastic as I was.

Maurice and Marguerite Hexter, solid middle-class Bostonians — country club members, no less — were going to become like those romantic creative Americans in Paris, Hemingway and Fitzgerald: *expatriates.* The idea did take a lot of getting used to. (When it comes to family, women are always more conservative than men.)

Still, it would be a great challenge and an exciting change. I was only thirty-eight and surely had enough resilience to undergo such an enormous professional shift.

When the time came for me to hand in my resignation at Federation, it was no great surprise. My activities in Zurich and my appointment to the Executive were well known. Harder was going to be my resignation from the Harvard faculty. I loved teaching and from time to time indulged in delightful daydreams in which I became a full-time professor at Harvard. The dreams would shatter when cold reality intruded with reminders of how meager faculty salaries were then.

First things first. We decided that the best place for my pregnant wife was back home in Milwaukee. In my daily phone talks with Felix Warburg — he was now chairman of the Administrative Committee of the Jewish Agency — I told him I was taking my wife by train to Milwaukee, and explained that she had had two miscarriages before. He paused a moment, then said, "I think I can help you there." As one of the richest men in America and a powerful financier with great influence with a number of railroads, he certainly could. Marguerite and I probably had the softest train ride anyone ever had between Boston and Milwaukee. We were ensconced in a large compartment on a train whose engineer had special instructions to *crawl* across other tracks to avoid undue vibration. We reached Chicago two and a half hours late, but the train to Milwaukee had been held for our arrival. In Milwaukee I took my wife to her family and quiet safety.

I returned to Boston and various winding-down operations. They should have been done without undue haste — after all, I wasn't expected in Jerusalem for a few months — but events in Palestine suddenly made everything much more hectic and pressing.

What intervened were the great Arab riots and murders in Palestine. Late in August 1929 Arabs armed with clubs, knives, and revolvers stormed the streets of Jerusalem, Hebron, and Safed. There were fewer than three hundred British police in the whole of Palestine, and many police were Arabs. They refused to fight their fellow Arabs, whether they were murdering innocents or not. Worse still, the British had recently refused a request to arm a large number of Jews for settlement protection. It took three bloody days before sufficient British army reinforcements were brought over from Egypt to quell the riots. Some 113 Jews were

Toward Palestine

killed and about 400 more seriously injured.

Immediately after the riots a worldwide Palestine Emergency Fund got under way to rebuild the damaged areas and provide relief for the wounded and for those widowed and orphaned in the Arab pogroms. More than $5 million was raised — the modern equivalent would be about $100 million. Now a delicate problem arose: The Jewish Agency wasn't yet a functioning body and the money was not going to be simply turned over to the Zionists. Somebody would have to direct the expenditure of the relief funds. Felix Warburg called me in Boston and told me I was going to be that somebody. He had conferred with David Brown, a New York banker who had been in charge of the American relief drive. It would be in addition to my work on the Executive of the Jewish Agency.

Late in September 1929, a day before Harvard was to open, I was in my office at Emerson Hall, which was next door to President Lowell's residence. I got a call from him: Could he come to see me? That was too much: I was a mere instructor, so I said politely, no, I'll come see you.

I walked over to his home. He said he had just gotten a call from Felix Warburg, who asked if I could be released from my Harvard duties so that I could go to Palestine to take charge of distributing the relief funds. Warburg told him I was particularly suitable because of my considerable experience in relief work during the Halifax harbor explosion of ammonium nitrate aboard a munitions ship in December 1917, when 1500 people were killed and 20,000 were made homeless. Social work relief teams from all over northeastern United States volunteered their help and I led a team from Cincinnati. (I suspect that Warburg laid it on a bit about my role, which was actually fairly modest.) Then Lowell clinched the matter: "Dr. Hexter, the University owes Felix Warburg and his father-in-law [Jacob H. Schiff of Kuhn, Loeb] so much for their generous gifts that we feel we can't refuse anything he asks of us. I've already spoken to Dr. Cabot [then head of the department I taught in] and he is willing to take over your courses." Put that way, of course, there was no way I couldn't accept.

The time span had shrunk drastically. Instead of months before I'd leave for Jerusalem, I now had only six weeks to tie up all the loose ends.

I had been in Boston just about ten years, a decade during which I had been able to effect major changes in the federation and its policies. Inevitably a testimonial dinner was arranged. It was a grand black tie affair at the Ritz-Carlton Hotel, with Louis E. Kirstein, president of federation, as toastmaster. Kirstein's opening was delightful: "To be perfectly honest with you, I am really very glad of the privilege of presiding at this dinner tonight. I am glad because I like Hexter. I have always liked him. I have liked him when he was not quite as fashionable [much laughter] and now that he is in fashion I like him just as well."

Felix Warburg had come up from New York for the occasion and his was the shortest talk. After defining my role to come in Palestine as being his "ear phone and mouthpiece there" he went on:

I feel like a thief before a Boston audience for the reason that I am taking Dr. Hexter away. I feel, however, that the need for a man of the unique type of Dr. Hexter in Palestine is far greater than the need for him in Boston. . . .

I assure Dr. Hexter that while he may not find in Palestine audiences of the same type and gatherings of the same size, he will nevertheless find problems which in their solution will be sufficiently interesting to compensate him for the loss of his Boston friends. The problems there are so great that, although I confess to being a thief, in view of the exigencies of the situation, I do it gladly. . . . If I had not believed he would succeed in it, I would not have uprooted him from his comfortable Boston environment. He goes with my full support, with all that means.

In my final reply to the encomiums I said that fortunately I had sense of humor and so was able to discount immediately 95 per cent of the things that had been said about me. "But even 5 per cent is an awful lot." I went on, with a smile, "I am really sorry that I caused all this trouble . . . I know how hard it is to get some of you out at night for meetings." I concluded that I felt this "was a great opportunity for high adventure . . . a chance to be in the swim and flux of history."

There was no point in adding that I was also engaging in a bit of thievery. Felix Warburg had said he was stealing me away. I, in turn, was stealing my secretary at Federation, Bessie Zuckrow. She was single, bright, and a fine secretary. It had been Warburg's idea. He felt certain that in the troubled atmosphere I would encounter in Jerusalem it would be imperative to have my own confidential, and trusted, secretary.

Marguerite couldn't be present, of course, so she had to be content with secondhand accounts — and the gift of a small diamond brooch from the dinner committee.

Before I was scheduled for a New York visit with Warburg I had a detour to Washington. Louis Dembitz Brandeis, the first Jew appointed to the United States Supreme Court, had invited me to spend a weekend with

Toward Palestine

him. I would have taken a much longer detour to spend time with the man who, in effect, had made Zionism respectable in the United States.

His German-Jewish family had come over in the 1840s and settled in Lexington, Kentucky, not far from my original neck of the woods. In time the family became thoroughly assimilated and had minimal Jewish ties. After brilliant studies at Harvard Law School he quickly became one of the most astute and highly paid lawyers in the country. He also had a great reputation as a reformer and as a confidant of President Wilson. In 1914, to everyone's surprise, he became the effective head of American Zionism, and in that role made it a much more efficient fund-raising organization than it had been before. He also pretty much took the steam out of the original attack by the anti-Zionists that the movement fostered divided loyalties. "Multiple loyalties are objectionable," he said, "only if they are inconsistent." He argued analogously, "every Irish-American who contributed toward advancing home rule for Ireland was a better man and a *better American for the sacrifices he made.*" And when he was nominated for the Supreme Court, he pointed out: "In the opinion of the President there is no conflict between Zionism and loyalty to America."

Like Herzl, another assimilated Jew, Brandeis had come to Zionism comparatively late in life. And when Brandeis went to Palestine right after the end of World War I he was greeted as a savior, a man who had made its survival during the war possible. At the end of his visit he said, "I know now why all the world wanted this land and why all peoples love it."

But among Jews here and in Europe many regarded him negatively. One critic said: "His entire conception of Zionism was *goyish* and not Jewish and this *goyish* concept of Zionism he wanted to impose on American Jewry." Why *goyish*? They felt he was more interested in efficiency, in accounting, in sound economic principles. He didn't have enough *passion* about Zionism; he didn't have a Yiddish heart. He wasn't as interested in awakening the *soul* of the Jewish people. In time, Weizmann's more mystical approach to Zionism won out. And now late in 1929 I was visiting Brandeis who had lost out to the Weizmann brand of Zionism.

An engaging conversationalist, he listened to my stories of what was going on in Boston, where he had lived many years, and offered advice on handling the relief funds. More important was his insight on how the Arabs were likely to react to the institution of the Jewish Agency directing Jewish affairs in Palestine. He was sure the Arabs would create a parallel institution, which would hasten further conflict. He was remarkably prescient. Our importation of nationalism into Palestine created, through some symbiotic process, a similar movement among Arabs and that led to the Arab Executive, which in turn exacerbated the conflict immensely.

In New York I was invited to stay at Felix Warburg's impressive mansion with its Gothic spires at Fifth Avenue and 92nd Street, facing the Central Park reservoir. (It is now the Jewish Museum.) In its day it was truly one of the extraordinary homes in the city, as befitted the residence of a most remarkable American. The six-story house opened to a large entrance hall with an adjoining "Etching Room" to house the Warburg print collection. The second floor had a full-scale electric pipe organ, which Warburg loved to play, and a "Red Room" for his Rembrandts and Botticellis and Raphaels. There was a huge conservatory and a formal dining room that could easily accommodate sixty diners. I was on the fifth floor, which had the squash court and my guest room.

Warburg had been born in Hamburg, Germany in 1871 and came to the United States in 1894. He married Jacob H. Schiff's daughter, Frieda, in a genuine love match. He became a partner in his father-in-law's banking firm, Kuhn, Loeb & Company, later rising to senior partner.

He was a very successful banker who helped in the economic and industrial transformation of the United States (Felix's older brother, Paul, was the truly serious banker. He was one of the main architects of the Federal Reserve System in the United States and later a Federal Reserve governor.)

Felix's real interests lay outside the Kuhn, Loeb offices at 52 William Street. He was interested in philanthropy—not only Jewish; education, culture, and music. (And romance. At eighteen, in Germany, he became the lover of Clara Schumann, the great pianist and widow of the composer. She was many years his senior. And now, though very happily married, Felix Warburg couldn't resist occasional flings.)

He was one of the richest Americans of his time and one of the few boxholders at the Metropolitan Opera the conductor would bow to when he appeared. He was also a Renaissance man. When I got to know him better I wasn't at all surprised to learn that he was probably the world's greatest expert on emeralds. He was also given to sudden enthusiasms: When his wife, Frieda, once suggested how nice it would be to have a cow or two at their Westchester Woodlands estate to provide fresh milk for the children, Warburg immediately acquired a Guernsey herd. The six hundred-acre estate also had a polo field, a squash court, and a set of black harness horses. The mansion was a Tudor affair with a large central tower, an indoor swimming pool, and a hothouse with orchids. And

Toward Palestine

a full Stradivarius string quartet.

I had first met Warburg in 1924, in an uncomfortable role. I had been delegated by fellow Jewish social workers to persuade him to change his mind about selecting the head of the new Graduate School of Jewish Social Work in New York, a pioneering institution. We recommended that he appoint Maurice Karpf, then superintendent of the Jewish Social Service Bureau of Chicago. Karpf, who was my age and had paralleled my career in many ways, was very able and widely respected. Somehow I convinced Warburg and Karpf was selected. Later Warburg told me that he remembered me for my "very effective advocacy."

Tall and handsome, Warburg was not an intellectual and not the smartest man in the world, but he had a rare quality denied to most of us: He was extraordinarily intuitive. His hunches on people, or situations, often didn't jibe with appearances or common sense, but 98 per cent of the time he was correct.

On my last day in New York I was scheduled to have lunch with Paul Baerwald, an old friend of Warburg's, and like him a German emigré. Baerwald, a partner in Lazard Frères, had been a founder of the great relief organization the Joint Distribution Committee. He was now its treasurer and Felix Warburg, chairman. The stock market had gone down sharply that week (this was September 1929) and Baerwald thought "the worst was over." So much for experts! (I was involved in a small way and not too concerned because the few stocks I held had been bought outright, rather than on margin. Fortunately I had never let my Boston broker, Lee Higginson, persuade me to invest in his favorite stock: Ivar Krueger, the Swedish match king. Krueger committed suicide and Higginson went out of business.)

That evening I had dinner at the Warburg mansion. He told me that among other things I was going abroad as his personal representative, empowered to commit him fully. To emphasize the commitment he had given me that morning at his office a letter of credit for $10,000 for expenses. (In today's terms and purchasing power, about $150,000.) That night at dinner there was a manila envelope under my plate with a note in it: "To be opened on the boat."

I was booked on the *Ile de France* — fully repaired now — and she usually departed at midnight. After dinner the Warburg limousine took me to the ship. I simply couldn't wait until I was aboard, so I opened the envelope in the car. It contained another letter of credit for $10,000 with a note explaining that it was for expenses that "you might be embarassed to put on the other letter of credit." Such splendid thoughtfulness and prescience. He could foresee situations where the money might have occasional sub rosa applications. He was right.

From the dock I phoned Marguerite to say good-by and to find out how her delicate pregnancy was proceeding. So far, so good. We spoke lightly of how lovely it would be when she and the baby could join me in Palestine — as if she was an ordinary expectant mother rather than a woman who had twice miscarried. So on this balmy night in September 1929 I left America for another world, another culture. A world where you went about armed and looked out constantly for enemies on the right and left. It was to be my home for the next decade.

The Atlantic crossing was exceptionally rough — a harbinger of things to come? We were eight hours late into Cherbourg and ten hours behind schedule into Southampton. I went to London and the Park Lane Hotel. Felix Warburg had urged that I get together immediately with Osmond d'Avigdor-Goldsmid, Simon Marks, and Lord Melchett. After a series of meetings we organized the structure of what we first called the Palestine Emergency Fund. I was selected as director of the fund, with an advisory committee consisting of Colonel Kisch, myself, and Pinhas Rutenberg, a Palestine engineer. Born in the Ukraine, Rutenberg came to Palestine in 1919. He had been active in forming a Jewish Legion during that war. In 1923 he founded the Palestine Electric Company, and was responsible for building the hydroelectric works in the Jordan valley. In 1928 he had been elected head of the Va'ad Leumi, or National Council of Palestine.

(During the course of these London meetings I got to know Simon Marks well and he suggested that it might be a good idea to buy stock in his Marks & Spencer retail chain. I followed his advice and did buy the shares — but sold them much too soon. I'd be a rich man today if I had held them.)

I got another financial tip in London: Letters of credit and crisp British banknotes are fine for every day, but in an emergency or under war threats the money to have in hand was gold — British gold sovereigns, then worth about five dollars each. It sounded sensible and before I left London I converted part of my letter of credit into one hundred gold sovereigns.

From London I went on to Berlin for a series of conferences with Max Warburg, Felix's older brother, who had stayed on in Hamburg to run the family banking firm of M. M. Warburg. These talks were about some confidential matters Felix had not wanted to write about. I spent a weekend at the Warburg country home outside Hamburg, which had its own golf course. On both sides of the Atlantic, the Warburgs lived very well.

Toward Palestine

Work

a photographic portfolio

The author at his desk in Emerson Hall, Harvard, 1924.

Typical settlement security building at Kibbutz Hefzi-Bah, Israel, served dual purpose of dining hall and security center in case of attack. It was erected by the Palestine Emergency Fund circa 1933.

School building at Kibbutz Tel-Adashim in 1935.

Hexter (at left) at newly erected settlement in the lower Galilee in 1935. The heliograph in the center was the principal means of communication with Haifa.

*Hexter and Dr. Arthur Ruppin of the Jewish Agency
at the Huleh Swamps in Israel, 1935.*

*One of the swimming pools at the Harry Kaufmann Campgrounds
of the Flora Haas Day Camp on Staten Island, N.Y.*

Grandchildren John and Terri with Maurice and Marjorie
at the Federation farewell dinner, 1967.

Marguerite, Maurice, and Marjorie at the same gala affair.

*Hartzfeld, Ben-Gurion, and Hexter at S'de Bokere, Israel
shortly before Ben-Gurion's death in 1973.*

*Hexter with Leonard Block (above) and Doris Rosenberg (at right)
at a MJA - Federation affair in 1987.*

The author laying a wreath on Ben-Gurion's grave in October, 1988.

5

A New Old World

ON MY WAY to Palestine I had been thinking of the problems I'd be facing on handling the Emergency Fund. Back in New York Felix Warburg and I decided it had to be totally separated from the Jewish Agency, of which I was now part. On the surface our decision would seem a harmless and practical principle, but in Palestine it became the subject of heated debate at the Jewish Agency before I had been there even a week.

Why? Because up to then all Jewish funds coming into Palestine had been subjected to the rule of "The Key"— the voting strength of the various political parties in at the last Zionist Congress. If the Labor party had 32 percent of the votes at the Congress, it would get 32 percent of all Keren Hayesod — later United Israel Appeal — money. "The Key" affected not only incoming funds: The rule also applied to allocating certificates of immigration, which the British administration granted the Jewish Agency twice annually. Without a certificate no immigrant could enter the country.

Naturally all the political parties attacked my revolutionary proposal. Everyone knew political parties lived on a diet of money, and here this newcomer from America was proposing to put them on a brand-new kind of fare. Fortunately, Pinhas Rutenberg agreed with me totally, and even Colonel Kisch, who was, after all, Weizmann's representative, wavered from the old line of "Key" distribution. So I won out on that rule.

I established a second principle: We weren't going to give alms; we were only going to give loans. I knew from my previous visit that the repayment psychology in Palestine was (as it still is) extremely high. There is

very little bad-debt write-off, because the debtor knows the repayment
is going to a national institution that will invest it in further projects in
the country, not for someone's private benefit.

Now we needed a hands-on administrator of the relief funds. I had
asked Rutenberg — by now an old Palestine hand — for suggestions. He
thought our best bet was Charles Passman, a bright, energetic American then living in Haifa. "Not only is he an honest man, but he is also
a local hero," Rutenberg told me.

Passman had come to Palestine in the early twenties from America,
where he had been an executive to represent an American syndicate, the
American Zion Commonwealth, to help develop the mandated territory. He had founded a city, Afula, below Nazareth, and was responsible
for the fantastic purchase from the Soursuk family of Beirut of the whole
of Haifa Bay. But soon the firm — which had $180,000 lent to it by Ameri-
can Zionists — went bankrupt. All the leaders dropped out except Passman, who acted as the local liquidator. He was meticulous and much was
saved for the stockholders. In gratitude they offered him a large piece of
the Haifa seashore. He told them the gratuity wasn't necessary; he was
a Zionist and did what was necessary. He doubtless kicked himself later,
Rutenberg went on, because that parcel of land later became worth millions of dollars.

Passman lived in Haifa and during the Arab riots of a few months earlier he had been in charge of the still-illegal local Haganah, the Jewish defense forces. He had saved the population of the Mount Carmel area with
a ruse. He had amassed about fifty empty oil drums and filled them with
stones, which are all over the area. When the attacking Arabs started
shooting their way up the mountain, Passman and his men released the
barrels in four different parts of the downward slopes. The noise the rolling barrels made sounded exactly like machine-gun and rifle fire and the
Arabs fled in panic. Yes, Rutenberg concluded, this is the man we need.
I met him, liked him, and he was appointed.

I had taken care of my own domestic arrangements by a stay in the
Pension Goldschmidt in Jerusalem. The Goldschmidts were orthodox and
their home cooking wasn't bad. There was only one restaurant in Jerusalem and it wasn't very good. In fact, at the time there wasn't a really good
restaurant in all Palestine. Hadassah Hospital had a very good cook and
you never turned down an invitation to visit the hospital for one business reason or another. But even Hadassah hadn't solved a nationwide
problem: There was no decent beef to be had in the land, only milk cows.

Another immediate problem was the language. The official meetings

A New Old World

of the Jewish Agency Executive were held on Sundays from 10:00 A.M. to 2:00 P.M., and were conducted in Hebrew. For my sake the secretary would translate key sections of the discussions. Obviously I'd have to start learning Hebrew in a hurry. Dr. Judah Magnes recommended the best teacher he knew, a Mr. Livni, and I arranged for him to come to my apartment every morning, except Saturday, from 7:00 to 9:00.

I had forgotten what little Hebrew I remembered from prayers in Cincinnati or from my bar mitzvah. I thought I had a time-saver: Instead of mastering the printed and written Hebrew letters I transformed them into English, using double consonants to replace certain of the letters I was being taught. It was a big mistake. Like all Semitic languages, Hebrew depends on two or three consonants with different vocalizations and in different combinations. To make matters worse the vowels are never printed or written, except in primers. Since the vowels form the basis of the moods and tenses . . . . There were lots of problems to overcome in those two-hour morning sessions. And my defective hearing magnified the difficulties.

Bessie Zuckrow, my secretary, had arrived and found quarters. There was a shortage of eligible women in Jerusalem, and I was sure that before long she'd have dates in the evening. Soon I met most of the other American expatriates like myself. Mostly they represented American charitable or cultural organizations. They provided a set of survival rules for life in Jerusalem and Palestine. It went something like this:

Remember Jerusalem is a *small* city. (The 1931 census figures showed a population of 90,000, with 51,000 Jews and 20,000 Muslims and 20,000 Christians.)

Watch the road carefully when you're driving your car. Arabs love to throw glass pieces in the street in the hope of giving you flat tires.

Water is precious here. Use it sparingly. (A good portion of Jerusalem still depended on cisterns for rainwater.)

I could expect to get an illness I had never heard of before, *popitachi*, which resulted from the bite of a sand fly. I'd get a fever for two or three days. Everybody got bitten sooner or later.

About the middle of March we'd have to live with the Khamsin, a hot southerly wind that blows for about fifty days. When it blew we'd have fine sand coming in even through closed windows and we'd be very uncomfortable. Work would be difficult. Everyone would be edgy, itchy, and suspicious.

And finally, since I was a heavy cigarette smoker — Palestine even had

Life Size

my Luckies available — I should know I risked life and limb if I smoked in the street on the Sabbath. The ultra-Orthodox roved the streets looking for sinners like me.

In spite of all these dire warnings my first weeks in Jerusalem were immensely stimulating. This ancient city sits on top of the central mountain-massif of the country and on a clear day you can see mountaintops many miles away. Here without feeling self-conscious you could reaffirm: I am a Jew — not a Zionist, not even a religious Jew — but a Jew, back in the very core of the land of our forefathers. It was an odd, heady feeling that would be heightened during the setting sun.

My first order of business was relief work. With Colonel Kisch and some guards we drove up to Hebron and Safed in the extreme north, which had endured most of the slaughter. The Arabs concentrated their attacks on the old, defenseless Jews, many of whom were descendants of families that had been in Palestine more than a thousand years. They hadn't believed in self-defense.

Colonel Kisch drew up plans for the town's reconstruction that would be built around a central security point, a fortified building that would hold the women and children in case of attack.

In Hebron the Yeshiva had been completely ruined and sixty-seven students and teachers slain. We immediately provided for the rebuilding. In the course of our visit I heard that a British newsreel photographer had taken several minutes of film of the destruction and the dead bodies lying scattered all over the place. Apparently it was too gruesome for the newsreel company to use. I sought him out in Jerusalem and bought the film from him and gave it to the Hebrew University archives. I didn't want our local hypernationalists, the Revisionists, to get their hands on the film and use it to further inflame *their* followers for a massacre of revenge. As far as I know it still lies buried in the archives. (The powerful memory of that terrible massacre still resonates today, sixty years later. In a recent Op-ed article in *The New York Times*, Meir Kahane, Israel's own wild man, talked about the terrible killing of the sixty-seven at Hebron that day in 1929.)

The basic assumption on the relief funds was that at the very least we had to redress the monetary damage individual families had suffered. What about the children whose parents had been killed? We provided for their maintenance until they were eighteen. One case I remember well was that of a little colony called Motza, just outside Jerusalem. Mr. and Mrs. Macleff were killed, as were four of their six children. The other two had been in a Jerusalem hospital at the time. We provided for them

A New Old World

until they were old enough to take care of themselves. The boy subsequently became chief of staff of the Israeli Army. He was only one of many outstanding "graduates" of our Widows and Orphans Fund.

Other necessary forms of relief included convalescent care or specialized treatment for the wounded who had been discharged from local hospitals. Those permanently disabled or invalided were trained for new occupations. Thousands of refugees from urban and rural areas received food, shelter, clothing, and medical care — some for many months. We had to set up temporary nurseries, schools, and recreational facilities. We had to provide emergency feeding of thousands of the Jerusalem poor who were unable to work during the disorders and for some time after. People who had filed claims with the government for property losses were given advances by the Emergency Fund. We also made loans — nearly all of which were repaid — to stores and businesses to keep them going. A special committee of local bankers and businessmen guided us on these loans. We also made loans to provide new housing in suburbs of Jerusalem and Haifa. In Safed we provided funds for the building of a commercial center, in reinforced concrete, on the site of the old Jewish quarter that had been destroyed.

These enormously varied relief tasks — we even arranged to provide tombstones for those who had been killed — kept me very busy. From the letters I received from Milwaukee I knew that everything was going well for Marguerite. With luck, she should give birth at the end of January 1930.

Anyone in charge of giving out relief funds is going to make enemies. And so I had — for not distributing the funds according to political party strength. The attacks took peculiar forms sometimes. Early in January 1930 I received a cable from Felix Warburg. Julius Rosenwald, a multimillionaire and prominent anti-Zionist, was going to be vacationing in Egypt. (In fact, it was to be a second honeymoon. He had married his son's mother-in-law.) I was given his arrival date in Cairo, and the name of his hotel. Warburg urged me to visit Rosenwald and persuade him to come to Palestine for a visit, even though both of us knew that Rosenwald had said publicly, "I shall not lift a finger to advance the immigration of Jews to Palestine, which has nothing to offer them." As it happened I had a meeting with Sir John Chancellor, the high commissioner for Palestine. I told him about Rosenwald, that I knew him fairly well and that he would at least listen to me.

Obviously if we could get Rosenwald to Palestine and show him around and "soften his heart" we *might* look forward to very large donations, which the country could use desperately. Sir John thought it was a fair chance and urged me to go. He even put his official plane and its pilot at my disposal for the trip to Cairo. (The only other way was a four-hour train journey.) I went out to the small airport near Lod, boarded the light plane, and was in Cairo in ninety minutes. I found Rosenwald and had a long talk with him, but couldn't budge him on his attitude to Palestine. I returned to Lod the next day. The daily paper, *Davar*, attacked me for spending Emergency Relief money on a "pleasure trip" to Cairo by airplane. How typical of an American outsider who wouldn't abide by local party traditions!

Fortunately, I was immediately defended in a long article by one of Palestine's most respected pioneers and labor leaders, Avraham Hartzfeld. We had met during my 1927 visit and became good friends. He was three years older than I was chronologically, decades older in experience. In 1910 in Russia he was sentenced to life imprisonment at hard labor in Siberia for being active in the Russian Socialist Zionist party. In 1914 he managed a fantastic escape from Siberia and somehow reached Palestine, where he worked as an agricultural laborer. During the First World War he organized an underground group that helped free Jews who had been arrested by the Turks, the occupying power. In 1920 he became one of the founders of the Histadrut and became a power in the Central Agricultural Council. He initiated many settlement projects.

He never married and had a very active social life. He seemed to have a female friend at just about every settlement he had helped create. He would usually leave his tiny apartment in Tel Aviv on a Sunday morning and come to Jerusalem with a little briefcase, in which he had a toothbrush and a pair of pajamas. He'd visit two or three settlements during the week — for inspection, advice, counseling — and be fed, housed and comforted by an attractive lady in residence. I doubt if he ever earned as much as fifty dollars a month in those years before World War II. But as he used to explain: "I don't need much. I have friends here and there." In spite of the differences between us he became my best friend. Whenever I am in Israel I visit his grave in Tiberias and think back on the extraordinary man he was.

The unpleasant *Davar* incident was offset greatly by the fact that just before I went out to the small Lod airport to fly to Cairo I was handed a cable just in from Milwaukee: I was the father of a healthy baby girl, and Marguerite was doing well. With such great news sustaining me I really couldn't get too excited about some nasty press libel.

Almost from the beginning of my Palestine stay I was faced with a dif-

A New Old World

ficult language problem. It wasn't Hebrew. It was the controversy over just what the word *executive* meant. In the United States the executive is generally a salaried appointee who serves at the will of the corporation's directors and is responsible to them. But the Executive of the Jewish Agency had a totally different view. Since they were the top elected representatives of the leading political parties they regarded themselves as the *final* decision makers, responsible to none except their parties. After our weekly four-hour session of the Executive on Sunday morning the party leaders would meet on Sunday night. From time to time they'd have to come back the following Sunday morning and say, "We've got too many objections from my other party leaders to this or that and we have to change it."

Felix Warburg finally learned to accept the very different concept of the executive in Jerusalem, but he never understood it. He once wrote me: "We have too many prima donnas and they all rehearse but do not sing; and when they open their mouths the sound is not pleasant." (As a major patron of the Metropolitan Opera he could have done something about *that*, but in Jerusalem his power was much more limited.)

There were far more serious problems facing Palestine and the Zionists. In London the government had appointed a commission to look into the causes of the 1929 Arab riots in Palestine. The Stanley Baldwin government had fallen in mid-1929 and was replaced by Prime Minister Ramsay MacDonald, who had appointed as the new colonial secretary Sidney Webb, a socialist who had been elevated to Lord Passfield. On the surface it would seem that Passfield would be quite sympathetic to his fellow socialists in Palestine — and there were a lot of them — but he and his wife, Beatrice Webb, were distinctly anti-Zionist. (Unfortunately they were also extremely gullible — just how much so was to be illustrated a few years later, when they issued an incredibly naïve book on Soviet communism and Stalin.) In any case, for the first time since the Balfour Declaration the Zionists faced a British colonial secretary who was far and away the most anti-Zionist official they ever had to deal with.

The commission held hearings in London and the Zionists were invited to have legal representation before the commission in order to present its viewpoints forcefully. A famous barrister was hired. He charged 1,000 guineas a day ($5,000), a truly fabulous sum that even Louis Marshall in his heyday wouldn't have dreamed of asking. Worse yet, the barrister felt he should have another lawyer in attendance and that turned out to be Lord Reading's barrister son, who was put on the legal payroll at 500 guineas a day. In all we spent more than £200,000 ($1 million) in legal expenses arguing a case that was unwinnable as long as Lord Pass-field was in control of the Colonial Office. (I'm pretty sure that Felix War-burg and Lord Melchett picked up most of the legal tab privately.)

Passfield had appointed a career colonial official, Sir Walter Shaw, who interpreted his mandate to explore the whole range of Arab objections to Zionism, not just the bloody riots of 1929. While his report did put the responsibility for the riots on the Arabs it also suggested firm meas-ures to prevent "excessive" immigration by Jews into Palestine. He recom-mended that another commission be appointed to see how many im-migrant Jews Palestine could accommodate. This was to be headed by Sir John Hope-Simpson.

Now, in one of the most terrible crises Zionism was facing, a Jewish Agency meeting was called for in London. Felix Warburg urged me to at-tend. A few days before I was to leave for the London meeting I got a ca-ble from Warburg: He had arranged for me to be picked up by the pilot who would be bringing in the S.S. *Europa* on her maiden voyage from New York to Cherbourg. I went to a certain quai in Cherbourg, where I was picked up 3:30 one morning, and we took the pilot's cutter out to the *Europa* at 5:00. The ship had already anchored and as we approached I could see on the navigation deck Felix Warburg, in a bathrobe, stand-ing next to the captain. With a megaphone Warburg yelled down to me that he had pictures of my new daughter, Marjorie. How did he get them? He had sent a photographer to Milwaukee to get the photos especially for this trip. I kept looking at the pictures over and over again on the trip to London. Not only did I have a beautiful baby girl but an employer who was extraordinarily generous and thoughtful.

The London meeting was concerned, of course, with the developing bitter anti-Zionism of Lord Passfield, but of even more immediate wor-ry was money. It was becoming clearer that the Wall Street crash wasn't a temporary aberration: A worldwide depression seemed to be setting in. A lot of major contributions pledged for Zionist causes in the States weren't being met. Retail business had been hit hard and a lot of middle-class Jewish proprietors had to reduce their pledges, too. As a result the Jewish Agency treasury was scraping bottom. The Keren-Hayesod — the fund for the developing of the land in Palestine — was broke and had to borrow money. At this point Felix Warburg's intuition came into play. The millions that had been collected for the Palestine Emergency Fund were resting in David Brown's New York bank, the Broadway National Bank and Trust Company. (Why this bank? Brown had been director of the Emergency Relief Fund.)

A New Old World

Brown was born in Scotland and was brought to Detroit as a child. He became a prominent businessman and Jewish community leader and in 1929 moved to New York, where he assumed control of the bank.

Now in London Felix Warburg was clearly uneasy about the Brown bank and felt that the millions in the account should be moved. (Several hundred thousand dollars had already been transferred to me in Jerusalem for the Rebuilding and Widows and Orphans funds.)

The delicate task of transferring the money to another bank, without insulting David Brown and his bank's soundness, was accomplished by a deft maneuver, pulled off by a private meeting of Felix Warburg, Lord Melchett, Chaim Weizmann, Dr. A. E. Wasserman, and myself. First Dr. Wasserman, head of the Deutsche Bank in Berlin, agreed to make a loan of $2,000,000 to the Jewish Agency. But there was a small hitch: Germany was then short of foreign exchange. So unless we were willing to draw upon this loan only to buy German products, such as irrigation pipe and the like, we'd be limited in using the loan. At this point Felix Warburg suggested that the three million dollars in David Brown's New York bank be transferred to Berlin. This account would be held in the name of the Palestine Emergency Fund and would in no way be linked to the loan by the bank. It was not collateral for the loan but would be a demand deposit that we could draw out any time we wanted to in dollars, regardless of how the Jewish Agency loan was being repaid. It was a clever move, but none of us could have foreseen the machiavellian maneuvers that would be called for in just two years to get the money out.

(Warburg's misgivings proved valid. In September 1930 Brown was forced out of his bank as chairman as the bank merged with two other trust companies in New York. All three disappeared by 1932.)

I returned to Palestine and the continuing work of the Emergency Fund. One day I was visited by Sir John Hope-Simpson, who was going to do a report for the British government. Were further restrictions needed on Jewish immigrants coming to Palestine? He had obviously decided that since I was a non-Zionist and represented American non-Zionists I might be susceptible to arguments for cutting back on immigration. I reported on our talks to my colleagues at our Sunday morning meetings. At our last talk Sir John asked me to help him finalize his report, which he was going to write in Athens.

During my London visit Felix Warburg and I discussed my future in Palestine. He wanted me to stay on for the long term, which of course meant bringing my wife and little Margie there. Now more than ever, he felt, he needed me there as his eyes and ears. My salary, as before, was to continue at fifteen thousand dollars, which in that early Depression year was generous.

Finally, in June, I was able to return to the States for a visit with Marguerite and our daughter. In Milwaukee I had the great joy of seeing my child for the first time — and sadness that arose because little Margie didn't know, or seem to care who I was. I laid out for Marguerite what living in Jerusalem would be — good and bad — and she was willing to try it, especially if we could take with us her able nurse, Mrs. Keske, a family friend. We arranged that Mrs. Keske would come with Marguerite and the baby to London for a few weeks and then join us in Palestine.

After a week in Milwaukee — seeing old friends, catching up on gossip of the Jewish community — I was cabled by the Colonial Office in London. Could I come as quickly as possible to Athens to help Sir John finalize his report? I cabled that I would and they arranged that once I got to Brindisi, Italy, they would fly me to Athens. A seaplane took me to Piraeus. The ensuing four days at the British Embassy in Athens were the severest I had ever gone through. I had to try to reason with a man who had already made up his mind. As far as he was concerned there just was "no room to swing a cat" in Palestine. I had facts and figures ready to show how every investment by world Jewry in Palestine served to provide new jobs for immigrants; how we had successfully uncovered and drilled for new water sources that made more agricultural colonies possible; how Rutenberg's electric generators had made it possible to create new industry; and on and on. He wouldn't be budged. Worse, he now began arguing that in all justice the Jewish money should go to unemployed Arabs. I said we had Jewish unemployed to care for, and added with emphasis that a number were unemployed because of Arab rioting, looting, and burning.

He was anxious for my approval of his document, but at the end of four days I told him with some severity that we were miles apart. That in no way could I approve his report.

Every night by phone or cable I kept the Zionist Organization in London informed of the talks, as I did with the Jewish Agency in Jerusalem. Obviously Sir John had hoped to inveigle me, a non-Zionist, into accepting his report, which *might* lull the Jewish community into accepting it. His obstinate mind set, his inability to see that it couldn't be acceptable, made it all too clear that we were in for a lengthy battle with the British government and Lord Passfield, our new enemy.

From Athens I took the train to Baden-Baden, where I was to meet Felix Warburg and his brother, Max, who were taking the waters there. One

A New Old World

night on the Orient Express, somewhere in Serbia, I was awakened by the Pullman porter who customarily took the passengers' passports so they wouldn't be awakened by customs and control officials at the borders. He said I was needed badly in an adjoining sleeping car, where a woman was giving birth. For a wild moment I looked at him blankly until it hit me that the passport had listed me as a *doctor* and teacher. It took a while to explain that there were doctors and doctors and I wasn't one who could be useful in the next car. So the train was delayed until a real doctor arrived and helped deliver the baby. As a result my train didn't arrive in Baden-Baden until 4:00 A.M. A hotel car had been waiting for me. After two nights and days on the sleeper I needed, most of all, a hot bath. I was soaking blissfully when the door suddenly opened and there stood Felix Warburg in a bathrobe. He said hello and what happened in Athens and I gave him a detailed account of the Hexter/Hope-Simpson exchanges in the steamy bathroom.

During the few days at the spa I renewed my friendship with Max Warburg, who was then one of Germany's premier bankers. Now that I was the father of a daughter he confided to me that he was worried about the free-and-easy ways of one of his daughters, Lola. I joked that just on the basis of her name she was doubly secure: Lo meant "no" in Hebrew; and "la" meant the same in Arabic. But nominal linguistics isn't much help in real life. Lola was reputed to have a fairly long affair with Chaim Weizmann, whose wife, Vera, had long become accustomed to his "flirtations."

After a few days of the spa, Felix Warburg and I went on to London to see Lord Passfield. Warburg and I had gone over several different approaches, but all of them were premised on a still reasonably open mind — and we knew that Passfield's hardened socialist heart had firmly turned against us.

We weren't surprised in London that we couldn't budge Passfield. Again I trotted out our facts and figures, which indicated that Palestine could safely absorb several hundred thousand Jewish immigrants with ease. It was no use. The Passfield White Paper on Palestine was issued shortly before the annual meeting of the Zionist Organization and the Jewish Agency. The effect of that document was so bitterly negative to the whole concept of Jewish settlement in Palestine and the original Balfour Declaration that Chaim Weizmann resigned. His entire philosophy of Zionism had rested on the fundamental support of the British government in implementing the Balfour Declaration.

The Passfield Paper was published on October 21, 1930. Since my reports on the Hope-Simpson talks that summer had been so pessimistic the Zionist Organization and Jewish Agency offices on Great Russell Street in London had been preparing for a counterattack. It was decided that I would be useful so I found an apartment in Queen Anne's Mansions for my family and nurse, who arrived a week before the paper was published.

The White Paper caused a great political brouhaha, which got the Labor government moving. It helped, I'm sure, that the humorless, priggish, doctrinaire Webbs weren't liked by most Labor members of Parliament. The Conservatives denounced the document as a breach of contract entered into when the Balfour Declaration had been accepted as a policy of the British government. Weizmann's resignation, followed by that of Felix Warburg and Lord Melchett, helped fuel the strenuous debates in Parliament. As the battle reached greater intensity Lord Passfield began backpedaling. *Perhaps* there were some points worth discussing with the Jewish Agency. Again I was brought in to the talks, and this time it was clear that Passfield was anxious to modify the White Paper; that he was now ready to listen to reason. It helped greatly that Prime Minister Ramsay MacDonald had been converted by Weizmann to a pro-Zionist viewpoint. In the end Passfield and his prejudices were defeated. In February 1931, the government repudiated the White Paper through the device of "explaining" its inner meanings. It reaffirmed the Zionist position fully.

The repudiation didn't come in time for Lord Melchett. He died right after Christmas 1930, at his home in Lowndes Square. His son, Henry, who succeeded him as Baron Melchett, asked me to teach him the Hebrew prayers for the dead. I was greatly touched that this young man, baptized and raised as a Christian, wanted to adhere to a Jewish tradition and recite the Kaddish.

Now that the emergency was more or less over it was safe to leave London for a little vacation in Switzerland, where father and daughter got to know each other better. We went from Switzerland to Venice, where we met Sir John and Lady Chancellor, the retiring high commissioner to Palestine.

In those days there was no landing dock facility at Jaffa harbor in Palestine. You descended from the large steamship to a small boat via a wobbly gangway. Marguerite went down the gangway carrying the baby. When she got to the last step an Arab took Margie from her arms without a word and threw her into the arms of his catcher in the bobbing boat. In time Marguerite got over her shock of how things were done in Palestine.

A New Old World

In Jerusalem we were temporary wayfarers, first at my old place, Pension Goldschmidt, and then in a borrowed apartment of Dr. Max Schlesinger of Hebrew University, whom I had known in Cincinnati. When he returned from vacation we found a small apartment near the Jewish Agency building where I had my office. Finally, the Hexter gypsies landed more firmly in a large furnished apartment in Rehavia. It was owned by an American lady and was very comfortable. We were able to hire a Polish-Jewish cook and housekeeper.

The accustomed manner of introducing a newcomer to the American Jewish community of Jerusalem was through the Saturday afternoon teas, when you went around from house to house, apartment to apartment, saying hello and *Gut Shabbas*. The other American expatriate ladies filled Marguerite in on the problems of shopping, health hints, and water.

Water was a precious commodity, to be used carefully and thoughtfully. In those days there was no pumping station to get water up from Ras-el-Ain, north of Tel Aviv, where the water supply of Jerusalem originated. So much of Jerusalem was primarily dependent on cisterns and rain, which was infrequent. If your cistern was running on dry you did without water or you bought it from Arabs who came around in carts filled with bulging water-laden sheepskins. Baths were a real trickle-down affair in the Hexter household. First our daughter was bathed, then Marguerite used the same water, then I did. Finally, the leftover water was used for our new dog and ultimately the floors got scrubbed.

In those days, before Jewish agriculture was organized enough to have farmers' markets in town, you generally bought vegetables in the Arab market. You never ate them raw, because the Arabs still used human feces as fertilizer. Before you cooked the vegetables you first soaked them in permangenate of potash.

The Arab riots of 1929 left everyone much more watchful. Jerusalem had no night life, let alone nightclubs, but it did have the Zion Cinema, which the American colony attended religiously every Saturday night. On other nights when I wasn't working my wife and I would listen on our new short-wave radio to the two main broadcasts from the States. (*The New York Times* would come in large batches — at least three weeks late. I wouldn't "peek" ahead; I'd read them according to date.)

Occasionally we'd go out for a walk at night, but we didn't go outside the invisible perimeter of the Jewish area. When we did I usually carried a revolver.

Members of the Jewish Agency had been empowered to carry revolvers or automatics for self-defense. This was a concession, because the Brit-

ish tried very hard to restrict the entry of arms into Palestine. But unknown to the British I also had a second gun. Why? Well, the British being
subject to change — as we had recently discovered — could very well re-
peal their revolver permit, in which event I'd still have a gun.

I would go for revolver practice at a makeshift range out at Kalendia,
where the Jerusalem airport is now. We used an extended one-hand stance
in those days, not the modern-day TV two-hand grip. I got to be a fairly
good shot.

In our search for protection many of us then in Palestine became the
beneficiaries of an unusual sequence of events that started at the University of Vienna during World War I. Two students met there. They were
Rudolf and Rudolfine, who sound like leads of a Viennese musical comedy. They had an unusual interest in common: boxer dogs. They fell in
love, graduated — he with a medical degree, she with a doctorate in
philosophy — and married. In 1920 they moved to the tiny village of Klein
Munchen, near Linz in Austria. There the Drs. Menzel bred a special kind
of boxer: one that obeyed commands quickly, almost instinctively, and
had marvelous trail-following abilities.

Their first sales were to police forces in Austria and gradually word
got around Europe that the Menzel boxers were very special. Orders for
their dogs increased. By a curious sequence news of these marvelous dogs
came to the attention of Eliyahu Golomb, leader of the Jewish Defense
in Palestine and main architect of the Haganah. (His brother-in-law was
Moshe Sharett, later to become Israel's first foreign minister.)

Golomb had come to Palestine in 1909. In 1918 he was a founder and
leading member of the movement to encourage volunteers for the Jewish Legion, in which he served as a corporal. After demobilization he
helped organize the underground Haganah. In 1922 he was sent abroad
to purchase arms and was arrested by the Viennese Police in July. He
wasn't held long but during his stay there he heard about the Menzels
and their great dogs. Even better, he discovered that the Menzels were
Jewish and quite enthusiastic about Zionism. Thus began the importation of the trained boxer dogs to Palestine.

In the Bible dogs are usually mentioned disparagingly, although shepherd and hunting dogs were approved. Arabs, on the other hand, regarded dogs as filthy animals and had nothing to do with them. In fact, most
Arabs were afraid of dogs. All of this Golomb knew, of course.

In 1936 the Menzels visited Palestine where their boxers were important security adjuncts in many settlements. Golomb and other Haganah
leaders took them around proudly. In 1938 the Menzels left Austria and

A New Old World

came to stay in Palestine, where they continued their dog training under the Palestine Canine Research Institute.

We had our own Menzel boxer, Thanatos (*death* in Greek). We liked him so much that we got him a mate, Cobra. We bred them and the pups were much sought after, fetching about one hundred dollars each. Their intelligence was high indeed and their protective instincts superb. I witnessed this one afternoon when I was walking little Margie in the street. In those days the Arab shepherds brought their goats and sheep into the street and sold their milk directly to customers. As Margie and I and the dog, on leash, were walking, one of the goats suddenly veered toward Margie. Thanatos broke his leash, leaped for the goat's jugular, and killed him instantly. (Obviously the goat meant no harm and the shepherd was minus a valuable animal, so I resolved the matter by paying him ten pounds.)

The dogs were specifically trained against Arab incursions and were taught to bark loudly whenever they heard the word *uskuth*, which means *quiet* in Arabic.

In the mornings I'd walk to the Jewish Agency office with Thanatos and once inside he'd jump atop the wooden file cases. When I was on the road he stayed at home to protect my wife and daughter. He exercised on the roof of the building we were in.

One Saturday morning I took Thanatos with me when I was shopping at the English store, Spinney. While waiting to be served I played with the dog and gave him his leash to hold. I gave him the command, *Tasik*, which in Hebrew meant, *Hold on tight*. An Arab in the store who had been watching me said he could easily get the dog to release the leash. I smiled and said, impossible. He insisted and bet me five pounds that he could. We went outside and he swung the animal by the leash ten times. I kept repeating "Tasik." Finally the exhausted Arab admitted defeat and paid up. As he looked back I said "Dayenu," and Thanatos released the leash as he had been taught.

Shortly after we were in our new apartment, I received a fine gift from Felix Warburg—a brand-new Packard ("Ask the man who owns one"). Staffers at the Jewish Agency said it was the only one of its kind in Palestine. I was congratulated, but some pointed out that it had a built-in liability: Its very conspicuousness could make me an Arab target.

You drove carefully, and if possible you didn't drive alone. Armed convoys ran once a day—except Saturday—from Haifa to Jerusalem and back, with two cars in front, an ambulance in the middle, and a couple of cars with soldiers in the back. There were larger convoys when a pas-

Life Size

senger ship came to Haifa. A lot of tough Arab terrain lay between Haifa and Jerusalem. The worst Arab rioting would come at the time of the Moslem holiday of Nebi Musa (the Prophet Moses), which generally coincided with Easter, and thus Passover.

Late in 1930, when I was nearly forty, I began learning lipreading from a Jerusalem teacher. It sounds ridiculous, put that baldly. How could a sensible partially deaf adult *not* have learned lipreading before this? Well, I had tried hearing aids but in the pre-electronic age they weren't very satisfactory. Generally, cupping my ear did as well as any hearing aid. I suppose that I was able to get away without lipreading because much of my adult life I was in a position to dispense funds to applicants. The people who sought money didn't seem to mind my saying: Please speak louder.

As my ability to read lips — in English and Hebrew — improved I began to reconsider other means of communication. Not so much for clarity as for safety.

My basic communication with New York and Felix Warburg would be a long letter I'd type — with two fingers — at home on Saturday mornings, on a Remington portable. Primarily, it would be an informed *digest* of the mass of material he was getting in New York: press releases, a précis on diplomatic maneuvering regarding Palestine, speeches of key individuals. A kind of news behind the news, I hoped. I'd also provide the week's activities at the agency; a brief list of activities by the Relief Fund, which was now concentrating on building new settlements and strengthening old ones; conflicts with the High Commissioner's office; changes, if any, in the local economy; and some personal tidbits.

These letters generally took three weeks to reach New York. If I had more urgent news I resorted to cable. My cable expenses were $50 to $100 a week, which came out of the $10,000 expense letter of credit Felix Warburg had given me. Most cables were sent clear but for the more sensitive ones we used one of the Bentley's commercial codes, which provided a book of nonsense five-letter units to replace the originals. Since anyone could buy a copy of the code "dictionary" you had to apply a secret transposition. For example, it wouldn't be an obvious word for word change — say, *emrig* for *government* — but you would use the date you sent the cable as the key. If you sent it on the third day of the month it meant you took the fourth word after *emrig* as your substitution for *government*. It was a nuisance.

If a matter was urgent or needed a delicate discussion where voice nuances were important I would take the four-hour train to Cairo and phone

A New Old World

New York from there. The trains left Palestine at 10:00 A.M. and returned at 4:00 P.M., which meant losing a whole working day. The call would cost anywhere from $50 to $100.

Things got complicated one day when my secretary discovered one of the Jewish Agency staffers going through papers on my desk. I warned that if it happened again there'd be firings, and I arranged that Warburg's letters to me should come to a box at the Jerusalem post office.

In one of his letters Felix Warburg wrote: "From what people tell me the mails are not absolutely safe and I would suggest that great care be taken."

(It is curious that while he suspected that letters to and from Jerusalem might be opened and read surreptitiously neither of us ever entertained a far likelier interception. Recently, someone who had wartime intelligence experience told me that before World War II the British *always* read all incoming and outgoing private cables in the colonies or where they simply controlled the cable company. If that was the situation I'm sure their cipher experts wouldn't have been stumped very long on our primitive substitutions in the Bentley Code.)

Inevitably we started getting sophisticated in the ways of secret communication. If nosy outsiders were reading our mail, we'd deliberately mislead them by planting false items. Life was beginning to get complicated when one day Dr. Werner Senator, the treasurer of the Jewish Agency, had a talk with me. We were very friendly — I had helped secure his appointment — and he had an interesting suggestion.

Senator, a short, bald, very competent Jewish communal official from Berlin, was a firm Zionist. He had been for many years the treasurer of the Joint Distribution Committee. He had a wealthy friend in Berlin, a Herr Schweitzer, who had made an investment in a curious machine invented by a suburban engineer named Arthur Scherbius. It was a code machine that couldn't be deciphered — except by one of its twins. The Germany navy bought one in 1928 and a year later so did an American named William Friedman, who was doing code work for the United States government. (Yes, the same Friedman who in 1941 broke the Japanese diplomatic code.) The machine was called Enigma and we could purchase it for about 1,000 German marks each, or about $250. Probably with a discount through Herr Schweitzer.

Since this was getting into fairly esoteric territory I sought to enlist the help of our military expert, Colonel Kisch. As I put it to him: "I have long been disturbed over the fact that doubtless our dispatches are not secret; you know how our codebook floats around on table tops. I have always been worried about certain of our letters which are vital to our interests falling into unfriendly hands."

I described the new machine: Werner Senator had given me a brochure on it. Colonel Kisch thought it might be a very good idea, and with that endorsement I brought the matter to Felix Warburg's attention. Clearly we'd need at least three machines: one in Jerusalem, another at the Zionist Organization in London, and a third in New York. In all, for less than $1,000, which I could easily have provided out of my own letter of credit. But Warburg wouldn't agree and the matter was dropped reluctantly. (A later, more complex variant of the Enigma machine was used by the British to break various German military and naval codes during World War II.)

I'm sure part of the objection to buying the machines was that it would require (a) training of trusted employees to operate the machines and (b) one person in each city to be able to *repair* the machine if there was a breakdown. It was not the kind of help you could expect from a neighborhood electrician. But I suspect that in Felix Warburg's mind there was another and far more important objection to getting the devices: the British reaction. If the Zionists and their allies were going to such great length to hide their communications they must be up to no good, or plotting God knows what. All of which might well make the British even less friendly, less cooperative. He probably decided it wasn't worth the risk. The turndown was a disappointment, but it was offset by a great surprise in the mail. It was a letter from him, dated January 2, 1931:

Dear Dr. Hexter:

By the time these lines reach you I hope to be some where in the warm south celebrating my 60th birthday. Looking back on the years that have gone, I see many difficult tasks lightened by your splendid cooperation and cheerful devotion.

Many people express only in their wills the admiration they have felt for their friends, but I should like to do it while I am alive. I do not know of a better time than now upon my turning this 60th corner, nor of a better way than sending you the enclosed check which has the "60" in it. I hope it will enable you to enjoy something which might otherwise felt you could not afford.

Very sincerely yours,

A New Old World

The check was for $6,000 and was totally unexpected. Who else gives presents on *his* birthday? I felt the Packard had been it for any lovely-surprise-of-the-year. I happily put an order in for one of those splendid mahogany-cased Capehart record players that played *both* sides of a 78-rpm record, the only kind we had then. The enormous variety and high quality of cultural and musical events that Israel enjoys today simply did not exist in the early thirties.

(The salutation and closing of the letter probably strike the modern reader as quaint. Such formality, such stiffness! It was several years before he'd commence his letters to me, Dear Maurice. And my letters to him were always, Dear Mr. Warburg. But he'd write to Weizmann as "Dear Chaim" and to Lord Melchett, "My dear Melchett.")

Before long my regular routine at the Jewish Agency was established. It went something like this:

Sunday from ten to two, at the weekly meeting of the Executive at the offices. Decisions would be discussed, finances reviewed, assignments made to each of us for troubleshooting. (I ran the Colonization Department.) Most Sundays, after the agency meeting we'd have lunch at home and then the family would go for a walk with Thanatos.

Monday would be a full day at the office. Dictating letters to my secretary. Handling phone calls. The phone service was only fair and we assumed that the British were listening in.

From Tuesday to Thursday evening I'd be out on the road visiting various colonies that the Relief Fund was helping rebuild or install new facilities. I'd take the Packard — usually with a guard-chauffeur, a man named Hershkowitz. We'd stay overnight in the colony we were visiting. Thursday night I'd spend in a Tel Aviv pension run by the Dan family, who later were to run a group of large hotels in Israel. Friday I'd be back at the office, which would close at 2:00 P.M.. By 2:30 the Naturei Karta Sabbath enforcers would be out in the streets tapping on shop windows: "Time to close down for Shabbas." (Marguerite got involved in volunteer work at the YMHA and some part-time teaching at the private Kallen School.)

Friday night we'd go out for dinner and usually met most of the other twenty or so other American families. Saturday mornings I'd be at home with my typewriter doing my weekly letter to Felix Warburg. In the afternoon we'd make the tea rounds at different American homes. And Saturday night we'd go to the Zion Cinema.

On July 4 the American colony would remind itself of its origins by

Life Size

playing baseball on a field up on the Nablus Road. Some of us tried to erect a tennis court in the heart of Rehavia, but as soon as the religious community learned that it would be used on Saturday, as well as the rest of the week, they raised holy hell and we couldn't get permission to build.

The orthodox even influenced our comings and goings. I got a cable from Weizmann in London that I would be needed there to brief Winston Churchill on various aspects of the Palestine situation in preparation for a parliamentary debate. This was Thursday and I'd have to be in London by Monday. Obviously the only way was to fly.

As it happened Imperial Airways, had just instituted a flying-boat service from India to England. The four-engined craft flew by day and rested at night. One of the stopping points was Lake Tiberias in Palestine. The plane left on Saturday morning and the next stop would be Athens, where the passengers would disembark for a hotel stay.

I had always respected orthodox sentiment and never did anything publicly that would irritate them. Even though I was practically a chain smoker I never lit a cigarette in public. Faced with this dilemma I went to see Rab Berlin, a colleague in the Executive. "To add to my problem," I said, "the plane leaves from Tiberias, one of the holy cities." He didn't understand at first; he *knew* that there was no airfield at Tiberias. I explained that this was a seaplane that landed on the sea of Kinneret.

He smiled. "That's simple, then. It's not a plane, it's a *boat*. You're allowed to be on a moving boat on a Saturday. Otherwise observing Jews could never have taken long journeys." So I arrived in London on a Monday without breaking Sabbath laws.

Jerusalem didn't get its first swimming pool until 1933, when the YMCA was built. Our first hotel with international standards, the King David, came in 1930. The first English language daily, the *Palestine Post* — later the *Jerusalem Post* — arrived in 1931. Not until 1936 did the Palestine Broadcasting Service begin giving us daily radio programs.

Most of us loved Jerusalem, but not everyone. One visitor referred to the "Jerusalem Sadness . . . the haughty and desolate beauty of a walled-in mountain fortress in the desert. . . . It is poisoned by holiness." But for most of us Jerusalem was the center of life in Palestine. Yes, we had too much sun and not enough rain, but we always consoled ourselves that things were much worse in Tel Aviv, on the coastal plain.

From time to time there'd be a fair amount of socializing with the British, and even the Arabs. Periodically there would be invitations to the High Commissioner's home and those of one or two higher-ranking British officials. Really, an exchange of polite dinners. Occasionally we'd meet

A New Old World

George Antonius and his wife. Antonius, a Christian, was the ablest of the Arab propagandists. His wife, a Moslem, was the daughter of the editor of an important Cairo daily. The couple entertained often and lavishly. She particularly favored younger officials in the various foreign consulates in Jerusalem. Things are never simple. Antonius also seemed to be very close to the wife of the German consul-general. She was Jewish but tried to hide it.

There were a few British Jews with important roles in the High Commissioner's Secretariat; and there were several Arabs, too. The British Civil Service Jews were almost equally divided — those who favored Zionism and those who didn't. Max Nurock, who was assistant chief secretary, had considerable power. He was an Irish Jew, a university graduate with a fine writing style who made no mystery of his Zionist sympathies. After Israel was established he became its first ambassador to Australia. On the other side was Albert M. Hyamson. When he came to Palestine in 1921 he was a Zionist, but by the mid-thirties he had become a rigid anti-Zionist. He was largely responsible for the narrow interpretation of the immigration quotas into Palestine.

And there was the official American, the United States consul general, George Wadsworth. He had joined the State Department after teaching at the American University at Beirut. He started as a consular clerk and worked his way up. His Arabic was fluent and sympathy for the Arab cause was apparent.

We exchanged visits. He'd give the current State Department official position on Palestine: very friendly. But from his words you could distill the bitterly anti-Zionist position of the department's Arabists, of which he was one. (The State Department anti-Zionist cabal probably was influential in preventing President Roosevelt from trying to get the British to allow more immigration into Palestine in the late thirties.)

Wadsworth knew that I was a non-Zionist oddly at work in a Zionist framework. I'm sure he often twisted my comments in his reports to the State Department, but his open Arab sympathies made him much less effective, I think. Still, we had to keep lines open to him: He was the highest-ranking American official in Palestine.

I had been far friendlier with his predecessor, Consul General Paul Knabenshue. He had once revealed a curious British attempt to enlist United States help to settle a vexing and dangerous Palestinian problem: the Wailing Wall, and who had the right to worship there. This was one of the factors in the 1929 Arab riots. The High Commissioner had asked the United States consul general to see if he could, through the State

Department, secure the services of Chief Justice Taft of the United States Supreme Court to come to Palestine and act as arbitrator on the Wailing Wall rights. I think the request simply died in the State Department files.

The one real friend I had in British officialdom was not a Briton. His name was Lewis Andrews, and he was an Australian who had fought with the British in the Near East in the First World War. He had stayed on to become District Commissioner of Galilee and Acre and then director of development. One of his great assets was a command of colloquial Arabic. He was also studying Hebrew. On my second or third meeting with him on colonization matters he smiled and said, "Remember, don't tell me anything I'd have to report to them." We became good friends after that. He was informal and funny and I got him to develop a liking for good bourbon. I was pretty sure he was part of a British secret intelligence network.

I had two interesting and useful Arab contacts whom I saw fairly regularly. One of them who lived in Gaza was Jamil Effendi el Shawwa, who sold us a lot of land. I became godfather to his son. He had a cousin who was a rabid anti-Zionist, a member of the Arab underground. One day Jamil visited me in Jerusalem and asked, very casually, if I was going to visit Gaza the following week. I said I was. He shook his head: It would be better to change my plans. I followed his advice and avoided being caught in an ambush of a convoy headed for Gaza.

My other main Arab contact was Ragheb Bey Nashashibi, the mayor of Jerusalem. He was also the leader of the party bearing his name. We worked with him when we could because his group was bitterly opposed to the other Arab political party, headed by Haj Amin el Husseini, the mufti of Jerusalem, and one of the most dangerous enemies Zionism had. This appointed religious leader promulgated the idea of a Jehad, or Holy War, against the Jews in Palestine. He was the first Arab to see anti-Semitism as a weapon against Zionism and the first to institute a boycott of all British *and* Jewish goods.

Haj Amin, the grand mufti, was a dangerous enemy and it was vital to try to get inside information on his plans. As it happened he had two cousins, privy to his plans, who also had a yen for Jewish girls. There were some attractive volunteers who dated the cousins and in the course of time we knew much of what the grand mufti was planning.

The opposed Arab groups fought bloodily. In one 1933 month 26 Arabs were killed and 187 injured in riots against the British in various cities. There were no Jewish casualties. (During World War II the exiled mufti became an ardent Nazi broadcaster from Berlin and is believed to

A New Old World

have played a small role in the planning of the Final Solution, the total destruction of European Jewry.)

On the old theory that the enemy of my enemy is my friend, it was important to keep good relations with Mayor Nashashibi. As it happened there was a chance to help the mayor a great deal — and to benefit the Jewish colony at Kalendia. The colony needed a steady supply of water and now that Jerusalem was reasonably well supplied I asked Nashashibi how we could get the water lines extended to Kalendia. I hinted that if he should cast his waters to the colony, bread would surely flow back. Fortunately, I had been prepared by the mayor's nephew, a first-class bastard, who knew I was going to see his uncle.

The nephew smiled crookedly: "Don't tell me you're going to see him empty-handed?"

I was still new at this business, and a little self-righteous: "I'm not bribing anybody."

The nephew laughed. "Who's talking bribes? Listen, do you play poker?" I said, of course. "Good, then next week we're going to arrange a friendly poker game, you, me, my uncle and one or two others. You're going to be a big loser — five thousand pounds — and my uncle is going to be the only big winner."

That's how Kalendia got water when it was finally brought up from the coastal plain. It was my first venture into bribery. I was soon to have a second. In Berlin.

6

Intrigue

SURROUNDED as we were by increasingly strident Arab nationalists, ready to boycott this month and kill the next, we were terribly embarrassed when a nonpolitical conflict broke out between two Jewish groups. From time to time members of the Executive would be called upon to handle some sudden emergency. My turn came about 3:00 on a Monday morning. I had to get over to Tel Aviv as quickly as possible and try to settle a nasty Jew-against-Jew battle.

It was a strike, a rare event then in Palestine, called by the newly organized orange pickers — nearly all Jewish — and the orange-grove owners, the *pardesanim*, all Jewish. (An orange grove is *pardes* in Hebrew. Stems from "paradise.") As it happened the British Colonial Secretary, Drummond Shields, was coming to visit Palestine and it was important that he not see Jew battling Jew over economic issues.

When I got to Tel Aviv I tried to arrange a meeting, but the grove owners were adamant: "We're not to face those so-and-sos under any circumstances." I promised they wouldn't have to *face* them. In a meeting room in the old Hertzlia School I arranged the rows of chairs so that they wouldn't have to look at one another while I stood in the center of the room and addressed both. I went through the opposing demands carefully and suggested a compromise solution, pointing out that if the oranges weren't picked some of the *pardesanim* would go broke, which meant that a lot of workers would be out of jobs, let alone a pay increase. As I talked some of them began turning around to face one another with a kind of sheepish smile. After several hours we had an agreement and so we didn't lose face before the distinguished British visitor.

We had avoided a Jew vs. Jew confrontation but we had to live with the knowledge that Arab vs. Jew skirmishes, or even battles, were inevitable, if the past was any guide. This meant that arms had to be obtained. Illegally, of course — the British didn't permit their import. I had, in code, discreetly queried Felix Warburg if it would be permitted to expend some of the Emergency Relief money on arms for the settlements. He said no, very firmly.

Chaim Weizmann now turned to Sir Osmond d'Avigdor-Goldsmid in London, an Emergency Fund director. Money was needed for arms. Sir Osmund — a tall, handsome fellow who had inherited his uncle's fortune on the condition that he add "Goldsmid" to his name — was all for using some money for arms but he was worried about violating the terms of the Defense Fund's legal status. He sought the opinion of another Jew, Lord Reading, a former Lord Chief Justice and Foreign Secretary in Ramsay MacDonald's coalition government of 1931. He said it would be a dangerous violation.

Still, in my visits to the colonies I could see that just having the new fortified centers wasn't enough. Eliyahu Golomb, the head of the underground Haganah, kept after me. They needed weapons to hold off any Arab invaders. I sounded out Paul Baerwald, head of the JDC in New York, asking if he could think of a couple of rich Jews who might be interested in supplying the colonists with certain implements not available from the British. Baerwald got the message quickly and he sounded out some prospects successfully. The Haganah got in touch with them. Before long some $50,000 was spent, mostly in Belgium and Czechoslovakia, on small arms, rifles, and machine guns. Many of them were smuggled into Palestine in cement barrels. I got involved in arranging payments to the arms makers and the shipping procedures. We used a little money, too, for some well-placed bribes at the customs house.

The world depression was deepening. Werner Senator, the Jewish Agency's treasurer in Jerusalem, was hard pressed to come up with needed funds and frequently had to issue notes — IOUs, really — for temporary loans from our local bankers, Barclay's. I used to kid him that he "was sowing his wild notes." But it was no joking matter, and all of us knew that at the World Zionist meeting in Switzerland in August money would be a major topic.

There was the Defense Fund money resting in a Berlin bank — the funds taken out of David Brown's bank in New York just in time. But the Deutsche Bank's hands were tied. There had been a sharp clampdown on foreign exchange in Germany and dollars or pounds could only be obtained through permission — seldom given — of a Foreign Exchange Control office in Berlin. We had a strong legal position: The original deposit had been made in dollars and it was stipulated that we could withdraw it in dollars. But a court fight was farthest from our minds. We were hard pressed and simply didn't have the time. Which meant direct action.

I went to Berlin in advance of the Zionist meeting in Switzerland. I learned that the official who controlled the Foreign Exchange office was a Graf von Hartenstein. The Hotel Bellevue where I was staying was a block from his office. We had a long, cordial talk — my German was still fluent — but he insisted he could do nothing. His hands were tied by the precise regulations.

There is a folklore about bribery. Basil Zaharoff, a contemporary of ours who was the world's great arms dealer, used to offer venal officials a few cigarettes. They were unusual in one special way: they were wrapped in high-denomination bank notes. Surely it couldn't be called a bribe. He had only offered the man some cigarettes!

A cute device, but it doesn't get to the heart of the problem: *Is the man bribable?* Zaharoff automatically assumed he was but now, in Berlin, I couldn't be sure. The man was a Prussian aristocrat but the Nazis were gaining in power and if he was one of them and a bribe was offered we could have a major scandal on our hands: *Foreign Jews Try to Corrupt Upright German Official!*

So I had to test. I put 1,000 German marks — about $250 — into a Hotel Bellevue envelope and called on the Graf in his office with the excuse that I had forgotten to give him some further data. As I got up to leave I dropped the envelope under it, and left.

It was an intense, anxious wait back at the hotel. If he called to say I had lost something in his office there obviously would be no deal. I waited twenty-four hours. He didn't phone. Then I arranged another meeting — in which there was still no mention of the envelope — and very gradually led up to the enormous inconvenience we were put to; how stricken people were being denied relief funds; how banking arrangements were being wiped out by unfair laws, and so on. Well, he said, perhaps something could be done. After all, you were promised that your dollar deposit would be always available in dollars. Still, it would be a matter of discussing the matter with other officials, persuading them . . . By this time it was clear that we were down to basics: how much? We finally worked out a deal for 5,000 gold sovereigns, even though England in September 1931 had gone off the gold standard. Still, it was a healthy $25,000

Intrigue

bribe — for which he would see to it that half of the original deposit, or $2.5 million, would be released in dollars. He gave me a document to take to the Deutsche Bank. I now went to the head of the bank, one of our great supporters, A. E. Wassermann. He was impressed with the document authorizing the release of half of our deposit. He smiled sadly. "The only difficulty is we have no dollars to give you." But he called some German Treasury officials and in a day or so we actually got the $2.5 million. In purchasing power we really got a lot more: The British had devalued the pound from $4.86 to $3.49, so the purchasing power of the dollar had, in effect, been increased by 28 per cent, as we would be converting the dollars into pounds for expenditure in Palestine.

The rest of the money on deposit we got out through the purchase of German supplies we could use in Palestine: irrigation pipe, motors, wiring. Badly needed materials. I reported to the agency Executive what I had done and I also cabled, in code, Felix Warburg in New York. Later when I saw him I started to provide the full details but he interrupted me quickly: "Shhh, shhh . . . I don't want to know anything about it."

At the annual World Zionist Congress in Switzerland that summer I was discreetly congratulated on the coup. At the meeting of the Jewish Agency Executive we were in the midst of a very long talk by Nahum Sokolow, a pioneer of Hebrew journalism and Zionism who was now president of the World Zionist Organization, since Chaim Weizmann's resignation in 1931. He was earnest and plodding and everyone was getting very restless. At the Executive there were no *short* talks; you started warming up after an hour's peroration. But now Sokolow was well into his second hour — and no one knew how, or dared, to stop him. Finally after ninety minutes I send him a little note in Hebrew. He interrupted his talk, read the note, and twenty seconds later concluded. My note read: "Your fly is open."

After the Congress ended, Marguerite, Margie, and I vacationed in Switzerland for a few weeks. I felt I had earned a well-deserved rest.

With the new money flowing in, I was now able to tackle some of my most ambitious colonization plans in Palestine.

For many years the southernmost colony in Palestine was Be'er Tuvia. It had been founded in 1882 by Jews from Bessarabia with Baron Rothschild money. It was not successful. Not enough water, too many Arabs surrounding them, and too many miles away from other Jewish colonies. After the 1929 riots the settlement was abandoned.

In those days the Zionist philosophy, which I fully supported, was that the Arabs should never be able to feel they had completely and terminally kicked us out of any settlement. It became my dream to recreate that colony — if we could find new water sources for irrigation. In discussing this with my good friend Avraham Hartzfeld we came up against one of the few disagreements we ever had on land policy. As a key member of the Central Agricultural Council — and one who was far more experienced in land settlements than I could ever be — he always commanded my attention and respect. But on this issue he found me unreasonably stubborn. Finally he gave in and we invested some money in water drilling. Fortunately, we found an ample supply of slightly saline water. Now we could begin. But again with a condition: I wanted to start a new policy on how we got a colony under way.

The old way was to start up a large number of colonies and gradually develop them. Very few new colonies were self-supporting. That meant they were living on relief work only — a drain on our funds that produced nothing useful. Gradually I won Hartzfeld over to doing things my way on a new kind of colony. If I was right we'd have a colony that would be self-supporting from Day One, instead of hovering between life and death for several miserable years. Suffering that way not only wasted people, and a lot of money, but ruined spirits as well.

The colonists we selected were particularly deserving of special attention. They were veterans of the Jewish Brigade that fought for the British in World War I. Among them were a considerable number of American Jews.

My plan called for the colonists to come down *after* we had erected the home, fully irrigated the land, and had the necessary structure and equipment in place. Each of the forty-four farm families got twenty-one acres. The Emergency Fund loaned them the money to buy the farms, with no repayment scheduled for the first five years; interest thereafter at a very modest 2 per cent. Their repayments went into a revolving fund to provide similar loans for more new colonies.

Be'er Tuvia became the most successful colony ever in Palestine and then in Israel: In fact, it helped make Israel possible. The existence of Be'er Tuvia, with its growing, armed population, saved Tel Aviv in the 1948 war. It was far and away the best investment we ever made with Emergency Relief money.

Today the settlement is probably the most prosperous in Israel. The original settlers and their descendants each had well-irrigated mixed-farming lands that produced great quantities of oranges, grapefruit, and cucumbers and supported lots of chickens and milk cows. Later, the set-

Intrigue

tlers moved from citrus to berries. Today each of the farms in the colony is probably worth $500,000. In their communal hall they have a plaque memorializing my role in the colony's creation. It makes me proud when I visit them, and a bit tearful.

After one of my Saturday morning letters to Warburg describing how well Be'er Tuvia was coming along he responded with a cable urging me to start thinking of an old-new source of colony financing. He meant the wealthiest Jewish foundation in the world: the ICA, the French acronym for the Jewish Colonization Association, generally known as *Icka*.

ICA started with one of those fascinating, larger-than-life figures that dot Jewish history. His name was Baron Maurice de Hirsch. His father had also been a baron and so had his grandfather, the first Jewish estate owner in Bavaria. A long line of court Jews.

Our Hirsch was born in 1831 and married into a prominent Jewish banking firm, but he didn't become a partner. He had another vision: the proposed Oriental Railway to link Constantinople with Vienna, which was to be financed by a Turkish lottery. Hirsch skillfully gained control of the concession — there was a lot of competition — and took charge of the project personally. His supervision and engineering insights made the project successful. It also made Hirsch one of the richest men in Europe. His contract called for a payment on a per-mile basis, which explains why the Orient Express today has such an irregular, almost meandering, route instead of a straight line. With his great profits he invested very success-fully in sugar and copper, so that by 1890 he had a fortune estimated at $100 million, making him one of the richest men in the world. (In today's dollars he'd be a billionaire.)

Hirsch became a socially prominent horse racer and hunter; an inti-mate of Edward VII when he was prince of Wales. When Lucien, his only child, died in 1887, Hirsch replied to a sympathy note with: "My son I have lost, but not my heir; humanity is my heir."

He proved it wasn't just a rhetorical flourish when he started on a long road of donations for special causes. During his railway-building period he became familiar with the daunting poverty of Jews in Eastern Europe. He started with a modest grant of $200,000 for trade schools for them. Then came the Baron de Hirsch Fund in New York for assisting im-migrants to the United States and Canada and finally, in 1891, the Jew-ish Colonization Association (ICA), to help mass migration of Jews from Russia to agricultural colonies in Argentina and Brazil. ICA purchased large tracts of land in various parts of North and South America for agricultural, commercial, and other purposes. He gave large sums to Lon-

Life Size

It was inevitable that Herzl would approach him for financing his dream of returning the Jews to Palestine. But Hirsch regarded Herzl as a hopeless visionary and refused any help. He was convinced the Jews could be fine farmers *if* they were provided with suitable conditions. "My personal experience," he wrote, "has led me to believe Jews have not lost the agricultural qualities their forefathers possessed. I shall try to make for them a new home in different lands, where as free farmers on their own soil, they can make themselves useful to the country." Anyplace but Palestine. When Hirsch died in 1896 his widow, Clara, continued her husband's philanthropic efforts and when she died in 1899 she left nearly all her fortune to various charities she and her husband had founded.

Before World War I, ICA had helped establish a couple of small colonies in Palestine, but these were mainly vine-growing farms that would produce wine. Since the Balfour Declaration there had been no ICA or Hirsch money coming into Palestine. Now, Felix Warburg felt was the time to get them interested again.

As it happened we had a friend at court. Sir Osmond d'Avigdor-Goldsmid, a member of the Emergency Fund board, was also on the ICA board. He passed me along to Sir Leonard Cohen, who was then president of ICA. (His son later became Lord Chief Justice of England.) Sir Leonard invited me to his estate near Cambridge to make my pitch. I had luncheon and afterward tried to persuade him that ICA should now get back in Palestine. Sir Leonard was adamant: Palestine was not an area ICA was interested in. When it got to be teatime I figured this was a lost cause and asked about the next train to London.

Mrs. Cohen, bless her, came up with a lovely note: "But Leonard, you can't let this young man go back to London without *something*." Sir Leonard looked at his wife and finally nodded. Perhaps, *something*. He would instruct the managing director of ICA in Paris to go out to Palestine and see what kind of farmers Jews were becoming.

In Paris I got together with the director, Louis Oungre, and invited him to come out to Palestine with his wife and daughter to see the marvelous agricultural achievements. Oungre, a Belgian Jew, was a lawyer who had a doctorate in philosophy. He was short, bald, and humorless, but honest and direct. Yes, he was willing to be shown.

In Palestine I introduced him to key members of the Executive and to Avraham Hartzfeld, who could talk agriculture with the best. We toured Jerusalem and he was impressed with the progress being made, but I knew that the only thing that might entice him — and ICA — would be

Intrigue

farming – preferably farming unto the second and third generation. (ICA was never happy with its Argentinean experience, because the sons lit out for the cities as soon as possible. A lot of their fathers did, too.) So I decided to take him down to Be'er Tuvia to show him our new model community. We couldn't go by car because there were no roads or bridges down there. We went on horseback. (I may have been a jockey once but my rear end had forgotten and I was sore for a week after.) When we got to Be'er Tuvia we passed a new barn and a small, very excited boy ran out. "Come in, come in," he shouted. "We've just had a new Holland calf born." Oungre led me into the barn, saw the calf, and began to weep. I was puzzled: "What are you crying about?" He wiped his eyes.

"That little boy . . . if a child can have such an interest in the birth of a calf then you have a real farming community here. I think ICA belongs in Palestine."

So a little boy became the persuasive argument for ICA funding in Palestine. He should surely be celebrated. And he was, but in quite a different fashion. He grew up to become General Israel Tal, leader of the victorious Israeli tank forces in the Sinai in the 1967 war. He later became chief of staff of the Israeli army and an international authority on tank warfare.

With Oungre won over, I wasn't going to propose any routine colonization plan with ICA. I had a vision of a huge territory in the north that could, under the right circumstances, provide thousands of new *dunams* of prime farm land. (A dunam is about a fourth of an acre.)

The area I had in mind was the Huleh valley. Today it is one of the most productive agricultural areas in Israel, producing record yields of wheat, cotton, peanuts, corn, flowers, vegetables, and fruits spread over more than twenty thousand acres. But when I toured it with Oungre it was simply a miserable valley hemmed in on three sides by fairly steep hills and mountain slopes in upper eastern Galilee. It was then mainly a shallow lake of about five square miles and about ten square miles of swamp. The malarial conditions in the area were so bad that the tiny Arab villages around the valley had the highest mortality rates and lowest living standards in all Palestine.

In 1912 two Beirut merchants got a concession from the Turks to drain the valley. Even though they never carried out their plan, the British upheld the concession. It was from these Beirut owners that ICA acquired the concession in 1934. We were helped greatly by my good friend Lewis Andrews, the District Commissioner for Galilee and probably the ablest man in the British Palestine service. But World War II intervened and it wasn't until 1951 that the drainage project got under way. It was concluded in 1958. At last, malaria was no longer a threat.

Since that first great breakthrough, most ICA grants now go to Israel for agricultural projects.

The year 1933 was a particularly memorable one, for me and for Palestine. For the Hexters it meant that we were definitely in Palestine for a stretch: We brought over our furniture from Boston and rented a large apartment on King George Street, (which local wits had long ago dubbed "Avinu Malkenu," a bilingual pun stemming from the High Holy Days prayer of "Avinu Malkenu," [Our Father, our King]). We had two bedrooms, a maid's room, kitchen, living room, parlor, dining room, and access to the roof where often we kept the dog. And a balcony, where little Margie loved to play. It was only 200 yards from the Jewish Agency offices.

The joy of being reunited with our familiar furniture and feeling less like gypsies was quickly dissipated with the cabled news that my mother was dying at the Jewish Hospital in Cincinnati. I had been sending my parents $150 a month regularly and her letters hadn't hinted at any serious illness. I asked Alice Emanuel, Felix Warburg's secretary, to check matters at the hospital. She cabled that mother had only a matter of days. Clearly there was no point in trying to make the three-week trip to get home. I got my old friend, Nathan Ransohoff to visit her, to explain why I couldn't get there. She told him she understood, that I had been a good boy and she was proud of what I was doing. That must have been reinforced by a telegram she got from Felix Warburg.

DEEPLY REGRET TO LEARN FROM YOUR SON OF YOUR ILLNESS. HE IS AT YOUR BEDSIDE IN THOUGHTS AND IS DISTRESSED THAT THE OCEAN SEPARATES HIM FROM YOU. MAY IT BE A CONSOLATION TO YOU THAT HE IS DOING A MARVELOUS PIECE OF WORK FOR HUMANITY IN A SPLENDID FASHION. HE HAS USED WISDOM TACT AND A SACRIFICING DEVOTION WHICH CALLS FORTH ADMIRATION FROM EVERYBODY.

She died three days later.

Intrigue

7

"Flashes Of The Infinite"

FOR PALESTINE 1933 marked a new stage of violence, between Jew and Jew.
I was awakened early one Saturday morning by the secretary of the Jewish Agency who told me that Chaim Arlosoroff had been shot and killed the night before in Tel Aviv. He had been born in Odessa in 1899. He was brilliant in six languages and a great orator. After a university education in Germany he became a Zionist and rose rapidly as a firm support of Weizmann. He was elected a member of the Jewish Agency Executive in 1931 with the special assignment to head the Political Department. (In effect, he did the final negotiations with the High Commissioner.)

He had been walking with his wife, Sima, on the beach in Tel Aviv when two men approached, flashed a light in his face, and one of them asked what time it was. Arlosoroff moved his hand toward his pocket watch. The stranger pulled out a handgun and fired a single shot, which in a few hours led to Arlo's death at Hadassah Hospital.

At first the evidence pointed to the Arabs, but gradually it became clear that the far likelier culprits were two Revisionists, who were identified by his widow. The two were tried and convicted but eventually freed by a higher court ruling that there was a lack of sufficient corroborating evidence. I've always been convinced of the guilt of the two Revisionists. They believed that moderates like "Arlo" were preventing Palestine from becoming a Jewish state "by steel and fire."

When I returned to Jerusalem after seeing Arlosoroff's body in the morgue I found a message that Menahem Ussishkin, a fellow member of the Executive, wanted to see me. He lived nearby and I walked over

on a Saturday afternoon. He said he wanted me to take over the politics
portfolio that Arlosoroff had held.

I was stunned. "You know I'm a non-Zionist. I'm not of the belief that all this belongs to us." He nodded. "That's why I want you. When Arlo went to the High Commissioner he talked for the Jewish people. When you go you won't be talking to him with *that* support. You'll have to come back and ask me and my political associates." No, I said, I'm not fit for that.

What made the proposal more unreal was that I didn't have a high regard for Ussishkin, whom some called the Iron Man of Russian Zionism. He was in many ways an impractical dreamer. He stormed his way through a couple of Sunday morning Executive meetings with a wild proposal: We should approach the Arabs to set up an exchange — we would take 100,000 Jews from Iraq and they would take 100,000 Arabs from Palestine.

There was another major development in 1933: It was the first year of the new increased Jewish immigration quotas. In protest, the Arabs staged a series of boycotts of British and Zionist goods. The year 1933 also saw sizable German emigration get under way, now that Hitler was in power. A lot of German Jews left their country that year, but most went elsewhere than Palestine.

Many of the German-Jewish immigrants to Palestine were able to bring some capital with them through an involved deal worked out by Max Warburg who, in spite of family pleas, insisted on staying on in Nazi Germany. He was convinced Hitler wouldn't last more than a year or so.

Another man of very fixed belief saw his dream come to fruition in 1933. His name was Moshe Novomeysky and like the others I met in Palestine who had a single goal in mind, he fascinated me. (Monomaniacs, someone has said, are the only true achievers.) Novomeysky achieved the successful extraction of minerals from the Dead Sea.

He grew up in Siberia, became involved in Zionism early, did some time in Czarist prisons, got a degree in mining engineering in Germany. There he first became interested in the potential of the Dead Sea, the ten-mile-wide salt sea on the border of Palestine and Transjordan. He settled in Palestine in 1920 and started work to get the concession to extract potash and bromides from the Dead Sea. It took ten years and much lobbying of Parliament in England before the Palestine Potash Company came into being. Now it was actually producing potash and bromine for export, and dream had become a real success. Novomeysky also founded a major fertilizer and chemical plant near Haifa. He was far and away

"Flashes of the Infinite"

one of the Palestine's most useful residents.

There were developments in the Hexter household now that we had our own furniture. I had received a huge package of 78-rpm classical records from the States, the Library of Music, which gave me great pleasure many evenings. (I had to play it loud because of my hearing impairment, but fortunately many of my neighbors also liked classical music.)

The Milwaukee woman we had brought out as our daughter's nurse had to return and we employed a Polish-Jewish girl, who had a fascinating Yiddish-English singsong intonation. We thought it might be a handicap if we eventually returned a child to America speaking English with a pronounced Yiddish accent. So on my trip back to the States I was able to bring back a teacher, Elizabeth Bingham, from the Shady Hill School in Cambridge. Her mother met me, approved, and Elizabeth came back to Palestine and became Margie's teacher until we returned to the States. She later became a teacher, and remained a family friend long after.

There were other changes. After the Arlo assassination all members of the Executive were assigned Haganah bodyguards. I had two assigned me, partly because my friend Lewis Andrews had gotten word from an informant inside the Arab ranks that I was on a hit list. I increased my revolver practice at the Kalendia shooting range to twice weekly. My bodyguards urged me to get rid of the big Packard — too conspicuous, they said. But we couldn't find another dependable car to replace it. So when I was in the Packard a guard was always with me. When I went out at night the guard would follow me and hang around until I returned home.

Laughter was in short supply, with reason. Those were grim times. A comedy troupe, "The Broom," that put on performances in Tel Aviv and Jerusalem couldn't make a go of it. But there was a kind of desperate humor, which the Germans call gallows humor (*Galgenhumor*). Some samples that I described in one of my Saturday morning letters to Felix Warburg:

> A very deep cellar is being dug beneath Government House so that the High Commissioner could express *very deep* regrets for future Arab riots.
>
> For a time during the Arab riots a 7:00 P.M. curfew was in effect. The joke went that all girls born next spring would be named Batsheba, after the biblical Jewess. Why? Because *sheeva* means seven, in Hebrew.
>
> For every Arab killed by the military, seven Arabs die laughing — at the ineptitude of the British forces.

Life Size

A *shadchen*, a marriage broker, took a pretty fifteen-year-old Jewish girl to the High Commissioner to make a match. He liked her looks but told the *shadchen* that she seemed a little young. The marriage broker smiled: "Don't worry. By the time you make up your mind she'll be old enough."

And there was humor in everyday life. Shmuel Dayan, the father of Moshe Dayan, was one of the first settlers in Nahalal. In the thirties he founded a school for German-Jewish girls, who were starting to come to Palestine in considerable number with their families. The object was to teach these city-bred girls how to be useful on a farm. One day they were sent to supervise the mating of a bull and a cow. An hour later they came back, very shamefacedly, to report failure. What happened? Dayan asked. "We couldn't get the cow to lie down."

By this time I knew the other members of the Executive very well, but the one I became closest to was a surprise to me, because my first impression of him was that he was a bully. It was Ben-Gurion.

He had steel-blue-gray eyes, red hair, and a stumpy body. Even for a short man his legs were small, but when he entered a room he brought a certain tenseness with him. He was a disturbing influence, and knew it. He very often lost his temper — on purpose.

Although my first impressions of him were negative he was one of the very few who welcomed me on the Executive when I came to join it in 1929. He said I'd have a lot of adjusting to do and he'd be glad to help me.

And he did. In time we became friends and fairly often he'd come to our apartment for luncheon and then a nap on the couch. He would also practice his halting English.

Ben-Gurion had come to Palestine in 1906 from Russia, where his father had been a provincial lawyer and notary. He worked for two years as an agricultural laborer before drifting into politics and the founding of the Histadrut, the General Federation of Jewish Labor in Palestine. Before World War I he had been briefly a law student in Constantinople and during the war he had fought with the Jewish Legion.

What fascinated me about him was that he had almost no interest in anything except politics. (Another monomaniac who achieved.) He certainly had no understanding of economics, and with it a lifelong lack of interest in money. He was not a religious Jew and he detested rabbis.

Ben-Gurion had a lot of firm opinions on his political opponents. He once told me he regarded Chaim Weizmann "as the most dangerous figure in Zionism." He was also quick to admit that the proportional

"Flashes of the Infinite"

representation voting plan adopted in Palestine was a terrible mistake. He now felt it gave minority parties too great an influence.

I don't think he ever had *close* friends. He was formal with everyone and there were aspects of his life no one penetrated, including his wife. He didn't seem to need anyone's love and affection. He simply knew what he wanted.

His education was spotty, but he taught himself just as he disciplined himself. I was curious to see that, like Felix Warburg, Ben-Gurion depended enormously on his intuition. In the end his qualities, good and bad, led him to win control of the Labor party and with that the premiership of the new state of Israel in 1948. With his control of the dominant Labor party he had defeated Chaim Weizmann, who was relegated to the largely ceremonial post of president of Israel, much to the surprise of Jews around the world who had heard much of Weizmann and little of Ben-Gurion.

In many ways the two were polar opposites. Weizmann was tall, with a commanding presence, and could play a crowd far better than Ben-Gurion. But B-G was a master in a committee meeting, where Weizmann was very bad. Weizmann had hypnotic eyes — rather like Rasputin's, I suspect. B-G's eyes never impressed me. Weizmann had lots of friends *and* admirers; Ben-Gurion had loads of admirers. Weizmann craved admiration; Ben-Gurion didn't. You could flatter Weizmann, never Ben-Gurion. If you flattered him, he knew you were lying.

Like all great men, Weizmann had his quirks. He always tried to avoid debating with an opponent who had a beard; Because he had such a beautiful mellow voice he was convinced that he would inevitably contract cancer of the throat. He was also a great and sometimes indiscreet chaser of attractive women.

Weizmann lived handsomely, almost royally. Not because of donations from wealthy Zionists, either. He had a large annual income from his chemical patents registered in the United States, Europe, Japan, and Australia. His large investment in the Marks & Spencer shares when they were first issued appreciated enormously. His magnificent London mansion in Addison Crescent was served by a butler, a chauffeur, a nurse-governess, a cook, and several maids. He always traveled first class, patronized only the best hotels, and was driven in a Rolls Royce. He smoked only the best cigars and all his suits were from Savile Row.

I was close to Ben-Gurion because we were at the Jewish Agency together in Jerusalem for many years. I would always meet with Weizmann when I was in London. He would ask my advice on colonization and the attitude of American Jews toward Zionism.

In the mid-thirties our setting up of new colonies had to be undertaken with the awareness that the Arabs would try to intervene. Thus was born the Stockade and Watchtower program (*Homa u-Migdal*, in Hebrew) in 1936. Most of these were large tracts of land the Jewish National Fund bought in areas far from Jewish population centers. The moves were carefully and secretly orchestrated. At daybreak armed convoys carrying hundreds of helpers, prefab huts, and electrical equipment would set out for the chosen area. On the scene there would be frenzied activity to get the houses up, and the settlement would be surrounded by a double wall of planks filled with stones and earth. In the center would be a searchlight tower and electric generator, so that night watches could be maintained.

To keep in touch on any Arab countermovements — there were no portable radio communications systems available — we'd arrange a series of heliograph stations — in effect, a series of mirrors that flashed the sun's rays in code. Most of these stockade and watchtower settlements were to the north of Haifa and inland.

We had a visit from Felix Warburg and his family in 1935. Among other things he had come to inspect the large one hundred-acre orange grove he had owned for many years. I took them around Palestine proudly to show the great progress since his last trip.

The Warburg visit took considerable behind-the-scenes arranging by the Jewish Agency Executive and the High Commissioner. There was always the distinct possibility that the Arabs might try to kidnap Felix Warburg to show their power. This wasn't Jewish paranoia — Arab ambushes and attacks *had* increased all over. On one of my recent trips to Tel Aviv I had passed a convalescent home called the Seven Sisters. Suddenly I heard a series of shots and a car about one hundred feet ahead veered violently off the road. The five Jews in the car were killed instantly. So now guards were placed all along the road the Warburg party traveled.

It was a fairly tense time, relieved at one point by a marvelous rustic misunderstanding. We had come to the Elizabeth Inn in Tiberias, a fairly good hotel. I had a room across the hall from Felix Warburg. In the morning, I heard a great commotion: he was shouting in German, English, and Spanish at an Arab servant, who clearly didn't understand a word. I asked what was wrong.

He said that the man returned a polished Warburg shoe and another that wasn't his. I nodded and explained that the man didn't understand a word he said so far. I turned to the servant and said in my newly acquired Arabic: "You brought the wrong shoe."

"Flashes of the Infinite"

He nodded. "My bad morning. That's the second time that's happened."

The Warburg party included his physician, who was also a friend. I began worrying a bit when I discovered that the doctor was also a heart specialist. Still, Felix Warburg seemed a normal, healthy sixty-four-year-old.

Besides the now thriving Be'er Tuvia colony we showed the Warburgs another proud project of the Emergency Fund. It had been conceived by my friend and coworker Avaraham Hartzfeld, which he called, in Hebrew, the Colonization of the Thousand. In effect, he proposed we set up small pieces of land attached to a house in the suburbs or rural section. Each tract, generally less than half an acre, was big enough for some chickens, a few orange trees, and a vegetable garden. The idea was that while the man of the house was working at his job his wife would care for the small tract and chickens.

Our only disagreement was how to select the families. Hartzfeld wanted to give the money to families that had what he called *staj*. What was *staj*? Seniority, families that had been around longer, possibly had better party connections. I opposed this, because I felt that since the wife was going to be in charge of the little project and working in the garden it is vital to select families which the wives were interested and *willing* to undertake the task. In the end we selected well and the program was a great success. We had a tremendously high repayment rate from the chosen families, partly because they knew the money was going to futher Zionist development and perhaps mainly because they were living better with their market gardens' fruit, vegetables, and eggs.

Meanwhile the rising Arab violence in Palestine led the British to send in twenty thousand additional troops, which caused the Arabs to call off a general strike. The violence also took a psychic toll in the Hexter family. From a letter to Warburg in May 1936: "The effect on children is sad. . . . Our little one had nightmares that Arabs have surrounded the house. She thinks every Arab is bad and wants to kill her. We've decided that next year she'll be sent to an American school. . . . We went to a movie last Saturday night—by good fortune not the one where three Jews were killed."

In an attempt to quiet matters the British halted further immigration and appointed yet another commission to study what was wrong in Palestine. It was to be headed by Viscount Peel. The commission came to Palestine late in 1936 and held numerous hearings through January 1937. Among other conclusions the commission said that Jewish immigration had benefited the whole country: "Much of the land had been sand dunes or swamps and uncultivated when purchased. Though today . . . the Arabs may denounce the vendors and regret the alienation of the land there was at the time of the earlier sales little evidence that the owners possessed either the resources or the training needed to develop the land."

Most of the hearings, which the Arabs initially boycotted, took place in the dining room of the Palace Hotel. There had been sixty-six meetings, of which thirty-one were public. Chaim Weizmann testified for three hours and so did all the members of the Executive and other Zionist leaders. Later there were fourteen Arab witnesses.

I was one of the witnesses heard in secret and my testimony ran about four hours. Mainly I showed them how, based on our intensive agricultural plans, the country could easily handle hundreds of thousands of immigrants. It was a tough session — rather like the grilling a Ph.D. candidate gets in his orals — and it came from British colonial and agricultural experts. You couldn't bull them. I explained our successful development of a new kind of irrigation, the slow-drip method, which makes it possible to use saline water. I pointed out that because of its climate Palestine could become a leading producer of what the French call *premier*, the first fresh fruits and vegetables that come on the market and always fetch a premium. (My prophecies have long since come true: The export of flowers, melons, and strawberries from Israel has become an enormous business.)

I was closely cross-examined by Sir Laurie Hammond, who had been the governor of Assam in India. At one stage of this grueling inquisition, Viscount Peel leaned over and said: "Won't you have a glass of water?"

"Yes," I said. "It may be the only thing I'm going to get here."

In fact we got more. The Peel Commission recommended a division of Palestine into Jewish and Arab states, a partition. It would have been a small state without the Negev, Beersheba, Haifa, or Jaffa. There were battles in the Executive and the Labor party, but in the end the Jewish Agency voted to accept the partition. "Klein aber mein" (small but mine) was the slogan. Barely. The proposed Jewish state would have had approximately 258,000 Jews and 225,000 Arabs.

The final vote by the Zionists would be made at the annual Zurich summer Congress of the World Zionist Organization. It was held from August 3 to 17. Weizmann worked hard to get at least conditional acceptance of the partition but the Revisionists and some of the hard-liners such as Ussishkin wouldn't go along: It had to be the whole of Palestine. Initially most delegates felt the same, but Weizmann's oratory and pleas prevailed and the partition was approved.

"Flashes of the Infinite"

All of this turned out to be an exercise in futility. At an Arab conference in September near Damascus the four hundred delegates voted *not* to accept the partition and demanded the end of the British mandate. With it came a real threat: "We must make Great Britain understand that she must choose between our friendship and the Jews. Britain must change her policy in Palestine or we shall be at liberty to side with other European powers whose policies are inimical to Great Britain."

I was with Felix Warburg much of the time in Zurich and for the first time it seemed to me that he had aged, that he didn't move with the old force. He seemed to tire more easily. He must have had premonitions. One night at dinner he handed me two sealed manila envelopes, each bearing the name of one of his friends. If "anything happened" I was to deliver the envelopes.

Back in Palestine Arab violence increased. One of the most serious casualties was my friend Lewis Andrews, the District Commissioner of Galilee.

He had been at a dinner party in Nablus on Saturday night and one of the guests noted that there were thirteen at table, which meant something "awful unlucky is going to happen to one of us." He said it was a pity Palestine didn't have a Paris institution called *quatorzièmes*, men and women who identified themselves with discreet signs that they were ready on short notice to make a fourteenth at dinner, in correct attire.

The next morning, September 26, 1937, Andrews went to the Anglican church services in Nazareth. When he came out an Arab gunman fired several shots that killed him on the church steps. In fact, he was on his way to meet me at Haifa dock on my arrival from Europe.

It was a terrible blow. He had been my good friend, and one who was sympathetic to Jewish aspirations in Palestine — which was surely why he was pinpointed for assassination.

Later the Andrews Memorial Hospital was planned in the Jewish colony of Nathaniya. In laying the foundation stone the High Commissioner, Sir Arthur Wauchope, said of his former adviser on Arab affairs: "He was a man who devoted his life to the good of the people, regardless of race or creed. No man was a closer friend, nor had I a wiser counselor in all Palestine . . . . Justice and uprighteousness were the keys to his character."

Andrews wasn't covered by any Colonial civil service pension scheme. His widow and three small children got one year's salary. Using my discretionary fund and that of some friends, I was able to add considerably to their income for several years.

Life Size

Five of the grand mufti's associates on the Arab Higher Committee — who were the probable instigators — were arrested and deported. The grand mufti himself fled, in disguise.

The next, even heavier blow came only three weeks after Andrew's assassination. A local newspaperman phoned me that he had just gotten a cable from New York that read simply: "Warburg died." Death came on October 20, 1937. I had tried to phone New York — we had just gotten international service from Jerusalem — but couldn't get through. Ironically, Warburg's last letter to me, October 16, 1937, had concluded with, "Don't be stingy with cables or telephone calls if things become hot. You are the only one there who keeps his head even if he doesn't keep his weight. Let me hear from you often but try not to let this thing touch your nerves too much."

There were several memorial services held in Jerusalem and elsewhere for a man who had been such a great benefactor of Palestine — one who had worked hard in its behalf even if he was a non-Zionist. At a hastily called memorial meeting in the Hall of the Jewish Agency building in Jerusalem I read a eulogy for him. It went, in part:

We have met to pay a last few words to a great man, a great Jew, a great American. Those of you who know my relationship to him will realize the tremendous difficulty I have in speaking. . . . In Zurich recently he reminded me that he was the last of the men who had formed the Joint Palestine Survey Committee and asked: When is my turn coming? . . . With his death there ends an epoch in American Jewish life. . . . For Palestine a great friend has passed on.

A few days later I had a letter from Sol Lowenstein, head of the Federation of Jewish Charities in New York. Would I *now* be interested in coming to New York and eventually taking over his job? (He had approached me twice before.) In my reply I wrote I was interested, and added: "I feel like a captain who has had to abandon his ship for a lifeboat with no compass. . . . The wrench is a very bitter one."

I accepted his invitation to come to New York during Christmas week to be interviewed by the Federation search committee. On my way I stopped off in London to see Sir Osmond d'Avigdor-Goldsmid, who was one of the four men directing the Emergency Fund and who was also president of the Jewish Colonization Association. He had been in poor health for some time so I went to see him at his country estate, Tonbridge. He asked if I would be interested in becoming Dr. Oungre's assistant, with

"Flashes of the Infinite"

a view toward succeeding him. I told him why I was going to New York. He said I'd be hearing from him.

I boarded the *Normandie* at Le Havre and went down for an early dinner. A middle-aged couple sat down at a table next to mine. While we were eating, my neighbor received a radiogram, showed it to his wife, then went looking for the chief steward, who promptly led him to my table. "You're Dr. Hexter, aren't you? I'm Lawrence Marks, president of Federation. I've just had this wire from Dr. Lowenstein saying you were aboard." We had long talks during the voyage.

When I got to New York I saw Dr. Lowenstein before the formal committee interview began. He was a little embarassed. "Maurice, are you hard of hearing?" I said, sure. "I never noticed it." I explained I had learned to read lips. He explained. "Marks said that when he walked on deck with you, you were brilliant but in the motion picture theatre you didn't understand anything he was saying . . . which I take it to mean you didn't understand a word he said in the dark."

The search committee consisted of Mrs. Arthur Lehman, Herman Block, Henry Ittleson, and Mrs. Sidney Borg. At the end of the meeting they invited me to take the job. I had already explained that I couldn't begin until the following July 1. There were many loose ends in Jerusalem.

I had been staying at the Warburg mansion on Fifth Avenue, as I usually did during my infrequent New York visits. Mrs. Warburg had cabled me that she expected me to continue doing so. After I had agreed to take the Federation job I got a call from Paul Baerwald, the veteran chairman of the Joint Distribution Committee and my secret accomplice in the early arming of the Haganah. He said he had to see me urgently. I went to his home on East 80th Street and he showed me a telegram that Carola Warburg, Felix's daughter, had received from Sir Osmond in which he begged Carola to insist that I accept the offer of the ICA. To sweeten it he said that I could combine that job in Europe with one at the JDC there, since Dr. Bernard Kahn, the director, was reaching retirement age. I told him I had already accepted the Federation offer.

I *had* been torn. If their offer had come two weeks earlier I would have been greatly tempted. Yes, a war in Europe was probably coming, but you could always get out. (I still had the gold sovereigns in my emergency kit.) But Marguerite was adamant. She wanted us back in America, away from Arab riots, nightmares, and threats of war. Regretfully, I had to agree with her. The charm of being expatriates had faded greatly.

While in New York I had a scheduled meeting with Fred Warburg, Felix's oldest son. He greeted me warmly and explained why he was anxious to see me. "Doc, we owe you a hell of a lot. You got Pop off that three-million-dollar liability in the Deutsche Bank affair and he was immensely grateful. He told us how you refused to accept pay for that service and he told us he'd square it with you, somehow. He did. He left you a nice bequest in his will." I returned the emergency gold sovereign hoard to the Warburgs.

Back in Jerusalem, there were several important decisions to make. First I had to provide continuity in running the Emergency Fund and the new relationship with the Jewish Colonization Association. Fortunately, I had a perfect choice available: Charles Passman. He had worked with me almost from the beginning on the Emergency Fund and he knew Palestine as well as anyone. I retained my board membership on the EMICA, which represented the joint operation of the Emergency Fund and ICA. (Years later, this was to lead to my present membership on the board of ICA itself.)

That done, my wife and I had to take care of the transfer of our furniture and belongings to New York. We used one of those big vans which German-Jewish refugees employed to bring their household equipment to Palestine.

The hardest part, as always, was saying good-by. There were farewell parties and teas and lots of handshakes and embraces. These were people with whom we had been through a great deal together.

The hardest partings were at the Executive at the Jewish Agency. These were men I had worked with — and argued with — for a decade. They were the men who would lead the State of Israel for many years.

There was a little party for me after our Sunday morning meeting on April 24, 1938. I made my parting talk, as I put it, "now that the sharp numbing surgery of good-by takes place."

By Executive standards it was a very short speech, perhaps ten minutes. Among other things, I said:

One cannot sit with men, even fight with them, for long years without engendering towards them a great measure of affection and regard. We must learn more how to differ strongly and still remain friends — otherwise democracy is unworkable. I have differed on many things as you know, many of them fundamental. It is the price perhaps of coming from an essentially different background, training and experience. I hope I have fought fairly; at any rate, I tried to.

I went on to say that I had been troubled by manifestations of the concept of force which I despised.

"Flashes of the Infinite"

I see in the concept force, of which there are seeds deeply sown, one of our greatest dangers. It is frightfully close to . . . totalitarianism and authoritarianism. As a minority group – or even as a small state – we Jews can exist only if the fundamental verities of a liberal life prevail. . . .

Am I deserting in a trying period? Inwardly the feeling is very strong and only overcome by the other feeling I have, rightly or wrongly, that I am impotent since the death of Mr. Warburg.

Now was the time to explain why I had long felt I was the odd man out in this company of strict party affiliation:

For good or for ill, there is no place in the dynamics of Palestine and especially at the center for the individual. I think it is for ill. . . . I come from the mythical West where "individual" still means something. . . . I come from a political milieu where the individual not a group is the su-mum bonum. . . . I cannot forget and abandon my judgment on affairs even though the group – the Executive – has taken a decision. That has been my greatest problem. . . . I have asked myself it it isn't inevitable that party developments . . . among us lead to the same end as elsewhere?

I got some laughs, too:

I came to Palestine with a total ignorance of Hebrew. It may interest you to know that I learned the word akshan *[stubborn] quickly. The word* pshara *[compromise] came much later. . . .*

And my great affection for Palestine will not lessen nor can the Hartz-felds, Dayans and Shertoks be forgotten.

I concluded that my years in Palestine had included "flashes of the infinite" in which I had seen this age-old dream become an eventual reality. But my stay had also included confirmation of the comment that there was no greater tragedy than when a beautiful theory met a stubborn fact.

Ben-Gurion responded for the Executive. He thanked me for all I had done for Palestine. While politically I was not of their views, he said, they respected those I held so deeply. He asked of me only one commitment: that I would not publicly campaign in America against the political views they held. I promised and in the years since I've kept my word, however much I wanted to protest this or that decision in Israel.

So I took my departure – the only non-Zionist to have been an integral part of the Executive of the Jewish Agency. Looking back, I can see that the years in Palestine had been the happiest of my life. In spite of the great problems and constant dangers, I have never felt so *alive.*

Our very leaving emphasized how prevalent violence had become in Palestine: We had to go from Jerusalem to Haifa in a protected convoy. In the middle were two Red Cross (Magen David) ambulances. There were guards in cars at either end. About halfway there was a shot fired at us. Marguerite hid little Margie in her lap in the back seat. I sat up front with two revolvers. It was touch and go until we got to the Jewish part of the Emek and from there to Haifa and the ship. I'm sure the journey confirmed Marguerite's view that it was definitely time to go home.

The Hexters and their governess/tutor, Elizabeth Bingham, returned to America by stages, with a lovely week in France, where I had to discuss matters with Oungre in Paris.

The nightmares didn't down the spirits of our daughter, but whooping cough did. Margie developed a severe cough on board the ship returning to the United States. Marguerite and I were pretty sure that it was whooping cough, which would mean quarantine for her on arrival. So we lied: We told the immigration inspectors who came aboard in New York harbor that little Margie wasn't with us because she was in the cabin with a bad case of diarrhea.

At forty-seven I was about to begin a new life. I was no longer an expatriate, merely a stranger in an America that had changed enormously since we left in 1929.

"Flashes of the Infinite"

8

Farewell Jerusalem, Hello New York

T HERE WERE SEVERAL shocks of relocation for which we were not prepared.

We got an apartment at 1155 Park Avenue, to which our much-traveled furniture came. But a lot took getting used to. We didn't need a guard dog. I wouldn't have to walk around with a loaded revolver. If I drove I wouldn't have to be on the lookout for glass deliberately strewn in the roadway. Little Margie probably wouldn't see another Arab for months, even years. And almost no one talked Hebrew. (We enrolled her in the Ethical Culture School.)

In our decade-long stay in Palestine the American government had been transformed. The New Deal agencies had made the government a much more intimate player in business and family life. Income taxes were a common topic of conversation. When we left in the late twenties, few people paid income taxes. Now, because I had arrived back in New York in June, six months of my Palestine earnings were taxable.

I got a humbling idea of just where I rated in New York when I reported for my first day at the old Federation building on West 47th Street, between Fifth and Sixth avenues, now the heart of the gold and diamond district.

Dr. Lowenstein used to get to his office early, so I arranged to be there a few minutes past eight and went up to his anteroom on the seventh floor to await him. I had been there five minutes when a tall, burly man burst into the room and demanded: "What the hell are you doing here and who

the hell let you in?" I said I was Maurice Hexter and I had an appointment with Dr. Lowenstein. He said, you wait downstairs, like everybody
else.

What a comedown! In Palestine I was known, respected — even if a
number of people didn't like me — and I was a member of the Executive,
the governing body for the Jews. Now I had turned into an unknown,
a nobody.

When Dr. Lowenstein came in I told him what happened. He called
the building superintendent who had ordered me out and explained who
I was. He was the most embarassed man I ever saw. He had been a Ma-
rine sergeant before he took over running the Federation building. (Later
we became friends, and I was helpful in getting him a pension when he
retired because of age.)

There were other shocks. I assumed that in time I would succeed Dr.
Lowenstein, who had already had one heart attack. The situation was
much cloudier. Someone else thought he was going to get Dr. Lowenstein's
job as head of Federation.

Joe Willen was brought to the United States from Russia when he was
eight. He served in the army in World War I and went to City College
of New York. He joined Federation as a clerk, worked hard, and rose
steadily on the fund-raising side. He invented or perfected several devices
now used routinely by all major charities. He invented the calling of cards
at the fund-raising dinners. (The man called would stand up and call out
the size of his contribution.) And Joe had perfected the organization of
donors by their trades or professions.

He had become the most professional, and most successful, fund raiser
in America. Federation's very low costs of raising money were the envy
of non-Jewish charities like the Red Cross and the March of Dimes. Understandably, Joe Willen had reason to believe that he might well succeed Lowenstein. Now I was there.

Dr. Lowenstein explained what had happened. The Federation trustees had concluded that while fund raising was vital there was another
badly needed element: somebody who had a lot of experience in the
spending of the funds raised. Spending it wisely, equitably, and with a
view to the future. That's why they had asked me to join Federation. The
old line was that two Jews can agree what a third should give. Now we
could add a rueful coda: All three of them could never agree on how much
every one of a couple of dozen agencies should get.

After Sol Lowenstein died in 1942 — on West 42nd Street, coming out
of a meeting of the State Department of Social Welfare — the question

Farewell Jerusalem, Hello New York

of just how the succession would work became a bit touchy. I had no formal commitment and hadn't asked for any, but still I thought I would be the heir apparent. I got the final word from Sam Leidesdorf, the treasurer of Federation: "We've decided, Maurice, that you're going to run the show. I hope you don't mind if we're giving the same title, executive vice-president, to Joe Willen, who will have charge of fund raising. You will have charge of everything else. In case of any trouble between you on jurisdiction, Joe knows that I will decide in your favor."

I had had enough of fund raising in Cincinnati, Milwaukee, and especially Boston. The idea that I would have almost nothing to do with that end made the job twice as attractive, even if I wasn't the nominal boss. It was the beginning of a long friendship and working partnership with Joe Willen. We were to have our disagreements and fights, God knows, but Joe and I always managed to return to a good working relationship.

With the basic relationship resolved it was now time to really look around at the enormous structure that Federation had become, particularly since it had recently absorbed the Brooklyn Federation of Jewish Charities.

That first summer I studied Federation and renewed old contacts with the Warburg family, particularly Frieda Warburg, Felix's widow. She was spending her summer, as usual, at their estate in Westchester. So was Sol Lowenstein, who had had a second heart attack and was taking it easy at one of the houses on the Warburg estate, Meadow Farm, which she now preferred to the older, adjoining baronial estate, Woodlands. (Felix Warburg had been the chief organizer and first president of Federation in 1917.)

At Federation headquarters in New York I followed the old advice that my mentor, Max Senior, had given me when I first began working in Jewish social work in Cincinnati. "Always study the old records. They're a gold mine of useful information." So I went through the minutes of the directors' meetings back to the founding.

Shortly after I had been in the job we had a major change. Lawrence Marx, Federation's president, whom I had met on the trip coming to New York, died suddenly. He was succeeded by Madeline Borg, an extremely handsome blue-eyed woman who was also quite remarkable. She was a widow. Her husband, Sidney, a banker, died in 1934. She never attended college but in 1912 she went to the children's court as a volunteer. Because of the lack of a probation staff for Jewish children she established the Jewish Big Sisters. After Federation was established in 1917 she became increasingly active. She really founded the Women's Division and was responsible for the spread of thrift shops around the country. She knew she was good-looking and could deal with men, so that she was a marvelous solicitor for major contributions. She was elected Federation's president in 1939, the first woman ever in that key post.

The first hot potato put in my lap was one that was going to influence medical education and hospitals all over the country. It started innocently enough with a visit from Leo Arnstein, president of Mt. Sinai Hospital, the oldest Jewish hospital in the United States. He had become a community leader not because of wealth — he was merely well-to-do — but because of his dedication and intelligence. Originally from San Francisco, he graduated from Yale in 1898 and in World War I was a lieutenant-colonel on the General Staff in Washington.

It seems that in 1938, before my arrival, the American Medical Association and the American Hospital Association had promulgated a major new rule for medical specialists. Up until then a doctor who had completed his medical training and clinical experience in internship or residency would hang out his shingle as a specialist in whatever area he thought would interest him (or produce more patients and fees). Now the medical authorities stipulated that after 1940 a physician would have to take tests before the appropriate specialty boards to qualify.

This was revolutionary stuff. It meant that in order to qualify, the doctor would have to train under acknowledged specialists who were now busy in private practice. In turn, this meant that all teaching hospitals, such as Mt. Sinai, would need a special appropriation to hire those specialists. In time I managed to wangle enough money for Mt. Sinai to commence such a program. But a lot of doctors were going to be very unhappy.

Why? Because the expensive full-time specialists came with a condition: They could have no paying patients. Private patients, if treated by them, paid the hospital. What's wrong with that? The chief surgeon of any hospital is the one who is going to get the top — and generally the best-paid — cases. Now, Mt. Sinai had two very able top surgeons who would lose a lot of those great operations if there was a new, full-time chief surgeon. Sure, he couldn't compete with them, but everyone wants the top man when a life is at stake — and, the two top part-time surgeons would suffer a great loss of income.

A great and cruel debate ensued at the hospital. Everybody was right, but there was no way of avoiding having a full-time chief surgeon if the hospital wanted to abide by the new rules. The debate got so hot for a

Farewell Jerusalem, Hello New York

time that if I had needed surgery then I probably would have had to go to a Boston hospital.

Another major development in Federation's outlook started innocently. Someone told me there was a woman in great need in Brooklyn and that nothing was being done for her. I phoned the head of the Jewish Family Agency in Brooklyn and told her what I had heard. She said, we'll take care of it. I didn't hear anything for a few weeks, when my original informant came by and said, nothing's been done. Again I phoned the head of the Brooklyn agency. "What happened?" She said the woman *hadn't come in*. I was puzzled. "Oh, we wrote to her, but she didn't come in." Again I got in touch with my informant, who gave a sad chuckle: "She's blind." This time the Brooklyn agency sent someone to see her, and helped greatly; and the case helped me break the back of a prevalent doctrine known as dynamic passivity. What did it mean? Your client could only be helped if he or she effectively *sought your help*: The needy family or individual has to seek out help or therapy. Workers would no longer go out to the needy, as in my day, when we didn't wait for them to come to us. Often the people who didn't come in had some extra self-respect and didn't want to become "needy," officially, which is what would happen if they sought out an agency for help.

As it happened, the Jewish Social Service Association had just begun concerning itself with another type of bashful client—the middle class. When I first heard the idea I was enthusiastic and a strong proponent of it thereafter. In essence what they set out to do was provide a fee-for-service center for middle-class people with all kinds of emotional, family, or child problems. They called it the Consultation Center, and kept it physically apart from the JSSA. Fees were a modest $1 to $3 per interview, and the idea spread quickly all over the country after World War II. Here, again, Federation was a midwife to innovation.

In my first month on the job I had managed to visit most of the 116 Federation agencies around the city, even the summer camps. And for the first time I realized how unusual Federation was, and how large. It certainly didn't resemble any of the other big-city Jewish federations I knew. The difference was that the New York version was started by the agencies and hospitals and they always intended to remain on top. How? There was a constitutional provision that the trustees sent to the central board by the agencies always numbered *twice* the number of the public trustees. The trustees representing the institutions would always be in the majority. Clearly they feared the power of a central financial institution with absolute authority. My first reaction was: My God, what a headache this is going to be when it comes to distributing funds! But in time I came to realize that it made sense, even if the central administration was often overruled by the agency directors.

I was helped greatly in those early days by the fact that the head of the Distribution Committee, Dr. Harry G. Friedman, was an old friend whom I had known well in Cincinnati. He too had gone to the University of Cincinnati and then gotten a doctorate in economics at Columbia, in 1908. He started his career as a statistician for the U.S. Labor Bureau and later became a specialist in gas and electric utilities. He was one of the founders of Federation and entered the Wall Street investment field, where he was very successful. To use an old-fashioned phrase, he was one of the noblest men I ever met. I don't think he had any enemies.

Also on the distribution committee, on the paid staff side, was Saul Cutler, who was a genius at figures and had a nose to smell out skullduggery in the budgets that all of the agencies used to get more money. Oddly enough, his efforts were not resented. In a way it showed that the agencies' directors and professional workers cared enough about what they were doing. If we turned them down they had another recourse.

Federation agencies retained the right to raise money from among their board members for their deficits or go to the community at large for endowments or for legacies. The trouble was that there often was great competition among agencies. Even though they were under the Federation umbrella some of them had the attitude of "mutual distrust tinged with apprehension." It was to give me and Federation trustees a lot of headaches.

Annually the agencies would submit on well-defined forms what they had spent in various areas, operations, and salaries. From these figures our Budget Department staff could determine the cost of an out-patient visit at Mount Sinai compared to one at Brooklyn Jewish Hospital. If an agency was efficient you praised it. If it wasn't it would learn how to become more efficient.

Occasionally, we'd turn up graft rather than mere inefficiency. In one of our hospitals we realized that pharmacy per capita costs had risen too sharply. The man in charge went to prison. Another time we found that the firm supplying several agencies with coffee was stealing us blind. We made him pay us back—with interest.

Understandably, the budget hearings, which were in effect the final watchdogs, were often hot and spirited. Budgets couldn't be cut by simply ruling that everything would be reduced by X percent. Some of our agencies got a large proportion of their internal revenue from patients and fees; others, such as community centers, had little or none, if they dealt with people who didn't pay or paid very little. On the Distribution Committee the rule was that no one could serve who was on the board of an agency or had a spouse who was on the board of an agency. We followed Justice Holmes's precept: "Not only must you be right, but you must seem to be right."

As I fell into the rhythm of the Federation year an unexpected detour came up. It stemmed from the Evian Conference of 1938, which had been convened by President Roosevelt to deal with the growing problem of Jewish refugees from Europe. Only one country of the thirty-two present offered to accept them: the Dominican Republic, which offered to take up to one hundred thousand refugees. The JDC (Joint Distribution Committee) promised a large sum in subsidies for the project. The Dominican Republic parliament had unanimously approved the immigrants freedom of religion and tax and customs exemptions. In turn the JDC and its recently created Dominican Republic Settlement Association (DORSA) promised a policy of selective immigration and financial support for the settlers.

Now in early 1940 JDC leaders came to me: Maurice, you're the colonization expert. Go down to the Dominican Republic and see what we have to do and make recommendations for its needs and future growth. I was willing, and Federation gave me three months' leave in the fall of 1940. I had been preceded by agricultural experts, headed by Dr. J. A. Rosen, a construction engineer, and two physicians.

Trujillo had given the JDC 22,300 acres of settlement near the town of Sosua on the north coast of the Dominican Republic. When World War II broke out there were only forty Jews in the entire country. By the time I got there in September 1940, the first settlers had begun trickling in. Wartime conditions made travel from Europe extremely difficult.

The land selected was an abandoned United Fruit plantation with several still-usable structures on it. I had done some reading before I went down and talked to a couple of Caribbean experts so that I knew something of the man I'd have to deal with, General Rafael Trujillo, president-dictator of the Dominican Republic.

My Mexican experience taught me that in Latin America people usually get into politics to make money. Trujillo was no exception. He had become far and away the richest man on the island. Back in 1773, when Clive of India was testifying before a parliamentary committee about his enormous take in the conquest of India, he capped the endless niggling queries about his loot with an indignant affirmation: "By God, Mr. Chairman, at this moment I stand astonished at my moderation."

Well, Trujillo was never moderate, but he was interesting. For one thing, he was the only Latin American dictator I ever heard of who instituted an effective literacy program. As a rule dictators don't want too many educated people around. Or as his fellow dictator, Salazar of Portugal, had put it: "It is education and undesirable literature, these are our enemies."

When I got to know Trujillo better I discovered why he had made the offer to take one hundred thousand Jews. It turned out that it was due to the kindness of a nice German-Jewish teenager at a Swiss finishing school in the early thirties. Trujillo's daughter, Flor de Oro, was a student there too, and was generally shunned by the others because of her dark complexion. Only the Jewish girl from Frankfurt befriended her. In 1937 when the Jewish girl and her family were seeking to leave Germany, Trujillo brought her, her family, and her new husband to Santiago in the Dominican Republic and installed the husband in the tobacco business, where he did very well.

Trujillo was a very able administrator who ran a fine cattle ranch. He could have been a great Latin America hero and leader if he had not been so greedy and bloody.

By 1942 there were only 472 Jewish settlers in Sosua. Few were farmers, or even inclined to be. Still, about 150 did go into farming, with the rest becoming businessmen or artisans of one kind or another. But the real value of Sosua was it saved more than five thousand Jewish lives. Trujillo had given us the right to issue Dominican Republic visas, which enabled a lot of Jews in occupied Europe to leave the Continent. So they went to Santo Domingo and then were able to move on to Canada or the United States. Without those visas they would have ended up in the death camps.

With the JDC loan funds the newcomers began building their own homes, a synagogue, a small power plant, an aqueduct, a school, and a clinic. Every now and then I had to remind myself that I was not back in Palestine again.

In the end the colony succeeded by accident. Oh, there were individual success stories. A Viennese baker became very prosperous. Jewish butchers from Germany and Austria bred cattle and developed meat and dairy farms that became well known all over the island. Their cheese and butter were first rate. The farms developed a variety of tomato that lent itself to export.

What put the finishing touch of success on the colony was air travel.

Farewell Jerusalem, Hello New York

When the colony was set up the island had only one airport, near the capital on the south coast. Now a new airport was built on the north coast, not far from Sosua. Land that the JDC had acquired by the hectare (two and a half acres) was sold in the subsequent land boom by the front foot. A lot of the original colonists became quite wealthy and moved to Miami. One of the colonists built two fine hotels in Sosua, and to this day when I go down in January for a couple of weeks he refuses to let me pay. The country gets a lot of tourists in the winter.

There were fascinating sidelights. Since there were many more male than female refugees there was a lot of intermarriage. Now Santo Dominicans are proud to claim Jewish blood. Down there you can be a Jew, a Mason, and a Catholic simultaneously. Of the original families that came in 1940 I believe only fifteen families and their descendants are still there. They were added to when Jewish immigrants from Shanghai arrived in 1947. The woman who was my cook during my 1940 stay later opened a restaurant that succeeded fabulously.

And the fiery daughter who had started it all by being befriended by a nice Jewish girl from Frankfurt? She was to become the darling of the tabloids with her many marriages and divorces. (Her third husband was a Jewish physician from Mt. Sinai Hospital. The marriage lasted less than a year.)

One day in 1943 I got a call at Federation from Trujillo. He begged me to do him a great favor. Flor de Ora was in a serious scrape in the States. Could I see what I could do to get her out of the country? He was sending a private plane to Teterboro Airport. Well, we owed him something. He had helped the Sosua settlers and another five thousand Jews. So I did what I could and that night I hustled her onto her father's plane at Teterboro. When I saw Trujillo after the war he embraced me and thrust a thick roll of one hundred dollar bills at me "for your splendid services." I thanked him and said I was glad to help the man who had helped so many Jews. No other reward was necessary. He was assassinated in 1961 after a thirty-one year period of absolute rule over his country. The man who killed Trujillo became head of the army there and lives in Sosua now. Sosua considers his presence a source of protection.

Not long after my return from a colonizing past I had another ghost turn up. It was Louis Oungre, the director of ICA, the Jewish Colonization Association, who had fled his Paris office before the Nazis entered Paris. I found him an office in the Federation building and every now and then when I'd pass him I'd marvel at the tricks of fate. If I had accepted the offer of Sir Osmond d'Avigdor-Goldsmid I'd be sitting in that office

Life Size

Federation for me.

One day I was handed one of Federation's long-festering problems by Sol Lowenstein. Two important Federation agencies had been feuding for years: the Hebrew Orphan Asylum and the Hebrew Sheltering Guardian Society, two very large child-care institutions.

Howard Lehman was head of the orphanage and Herman Bloch of the Guardian group. For years Federation had tried to get these two groups to merge, not simply for economy but to end the unseemly competition between them. The rivalry would come to a head when they battled each other at the City Welfare Department of Children.

They were fighting for bodies. When you run an institution the largest deficit is caused by a vacant bed, not by an occupied one. So these rivals, each of which had a boarding-out service as well as institutional services, wanted to keep their client populations at 100 per cent. That led to intense competition for orphaned or abandoned children and a too-severe attitude about their dismissal. They didn't like to send a child home until a replacement was found.

Things got so bad that the New York welfare commissioner had called on Federation to arrange an orderly allocation of children. For years attempts had been made, quite futilely, to merge. Now Howard Lehman and Herman Bloch came to Sol Lowenstein and said that if Hexter took charge they'd support whatever changes I wanted.

I studied the history of both institutions. The Hebrew Orphan Asylum, started in 1830, had the distinction of being the oldest Jewish philanthropic institution in the city. It had a very large building at 137th Street and Amsterdam Avenue, near City College. It had been the beneficiary of a million-dollar grant from Federation's first building fund campaign in 1919 — a huge sum for those days. They also had a boarding-out setup and an institution for retarded children.

The Hebrew Sheltering Guardian Society was a newer group spawned largely by Sam Lewisohn, a charter member of "Our Crowd." His institution had gone out to Pleasantville, New York. Instead of having one very large building, as the Hebrew Orphan group did, they had a series of cottages, each with its own "parents." Twenty to twenty-six children occupied each cottage, with a trained couple in charge. They tried to resemble family life as much as possible.

They also had a remarkable woman, Mary Boretz, who had devised the foster-care program. Instead of automatically sending children to an institution she first sought to find families to take care of them for a monthly fee. She was a great pioneer.

Between them the two institutions had 4,600 children, with about 1,000 children "inside" and the bulk in foster homes. So the first task was to reduce the number of children still inside. Using the criteria Mary Boretz originated, I was able to put more children into approved foster care. The heart of the change would be the central intake bureau, which would decide which institution a child should be sent to. This meant stepping on a lot of social-work toes.

Visiting the Westchester society to observe a session at which it was decided which child would go to which cottage — trying to match cottage parents' attitudes with the child's — I was drawn to a young social worker because of the reasoning behind her decisions. I addressed the assembled social workers up there and announced bluntly that they in Westchester and their colleagues at the Orphan Asylum in New York were working for *one* new institution and I proposed to make some personnel shifts. Among other changes I assigned the bright social worker, Martha Selig, to a central intake service. She said she didn't think she wanted to do that. I said, when do you want to resign? She didn't want to resign and I laid down the law: "If you want to work here you're going where I want you to go." She finally did, and went on to become one of the leading social workers in New York. Later I made her one of my assistants at Federation.

The intake service was key to the merger. It alone could make a diagnostic study of the child and determine which was the best place for it. In effect, the two big institutions had lost their autonomy because the intake service made or broke an agency. Even on dismissal of a child from supervision the intake service was the final authority.

The result was that our census shrank by 60 per cent in the first year of the new operation. We found that children had been kept away from their families unnecessarily. Year by year the orphanage population fell and when it had less than 150 children I said the dirty words: Maybe it's time to close the orphanage.

I showed the directors that we could keep the children in the Ritz-Carlton Hotel for less than it cost us to maintain them in that huge building. The temperature in the room dropped 30 degrees in five minutes. One of the directors, a man named Saul Driben who had risen from office boy to a multimillionaire in the textile business, challenged me. "What do you know about this institution? I've been coming here every week for years.

Life Size

And now you come along and say we ought to close it. What do you know?"

"Mr. Driben, you know this institution from the top to bottom?"

"Yes, I do."

"How many mattresses are there on each child's cot?"

"One."

"Would it surprise you to learn they have *none*? They use blankets, because if a child wet his bed the mattress couldn't be cleaned but blankets could."

He was embarassed and said he wanted to think things over. Finally, in 1941, we arranged to sell the orphan asylum to the city for $1.4 million, a very good price that we arrived at with the help of a man in the city's real estate department. We got to talking and when he learned I had lived in Palestine for ten years he smiled and said in Hebrew, *Ani imcha*, I'm with you. Great, I said. How much should we ask for?

"Ask for two million," he suggested. We had been thinking of much, much less. I asked why so much. He smiled: "The city has been buying Catholic institutions for very good prices. They have gotten used to paying good money. So ask." We finally got bargained down to the $1.4 million, much more than we expected.

Before the merger was closed there was the matter of a name for the combined institutions. Each organization wanted its name first in the result and somebody suggested a meld, the Hebrew Orphan Guardian Society. Everyone seemed to like it until I laughed. "Can you see the combined bands of the two institutions marching in a parade? Can you see the initials of the institution on the big drums: H-O-G-S . . . Hogs and Jewish children?" That killed that suggestion and eventually they agreed on a neutral Jewish Child Care Association.

(The orphanage's closing involved real pain for Saul Driben. "Now I won't have a place to go to every week," he said dolefully.)

As the merger became effective there was still a nagging situation that none of us wanted to think about because it was a peculiar mess. But since I had been appointed heavy-duty cleanup man I had to get to it.

The two big child-care institutions did not take infants. We had another organization for that, the Home for Hebrew Infants, up in the Bronx. They had resisted coming into the merger, for an odd reason.

In 1907 Isadore Stettenheim, who made a lot of money in the insurance business, gave the Home for Hebrew Infants fifty thousand dollars to put up a building in memory of a dead son. He stipulated that the build-

Farewell Jerusalem, Hello New York

ing would *always* carry the name of his son and that if it ever burned down or moved the building would be replaced, with its name intact — in effect, a covenant running with the land that meant the land couldn't be sold without satisfying that covenant. The trouble was that in 1907 he — nor anybody else that matter — could foresee a time when such institutions would outlive their original function.

(One of the wisest Americans, Benjamin Franklin, had a similar limited vision. His will set up two trust funds with about five thousand dollars each in Philadelphia and Boston to be lent out at 5 per cent to "young married artificers" under twenty-five who had served their apprenticeships. The loans would enable them to set up their own businesses. The trusts were to run two hundred years. After 1885 the trustees couldn't find any applicants and by 1908 the funds had grown to $175,000.)

During the struggle to merge the child-care institutions Stettenheim grew enraged and stopped making his annual twenty-five thousand dollar gift to Federation. Actually, it was from a foundation that he had set up in the name of his first wife. Now he was remarried, to Walter Lippman's widowed mother, Daisy. This complicated matters, because the new Mrs. Stettenheim resented the fund named after Stettenheim's first wife. She insisted on its liquidation. (There's some bitter social comedy here, too. Lippman, the renowned columnist, resented his Jewish birth, disliked his mother — he paid a duty call on her once a year — and probably was enraged that he was now the stepson of an Isadore Stettenheim. "The rich and vulgar and pretentious Jews of our big American cities are perhaps the greatest misfortune that has ever befallen the Jewish people," he wrote. "They are the real fount of anti-Semitism.")

Four years had gone by and Federation had not gotten the $100,000 that the Stettenheim Foundation had promised to contribute in that period. The situation had to be resolved, so I visited him at his elegant apartment on Fifth Avenue. I told him I thought he had been shamefully treated and that we were going to return his original $50,000 building fund gift he had made in 1907. I said of course we would expect him to become a regular contributor again. He said, on reflection, "You're the first decent fellow who's come to see me. You've got a deal." He gave us the past-due $100,000 and added a provision to his foundation charter that called for it to continue paying the $25,000 a year.

When his second wife, Daisy, died he wanted to liquidate his foundation, but there was that new provision for Federation. What to do? Eventually we worked out a deal: he'd give a lump sum of $300,000 to Federation and wipe out the foundation's obligation to us. In turn the money

Life Size

became an important part of the wealth of the Jewish Child Care Association. The original building of the Home for Hebrew Infants was converted into the Hebrew Home for Aged.

These special assignments handed me were above and beyond the normal course of my duties at Federation. A year's routine went something like this:

I'd be in my office at 8:00 A.M. Early in January the budgetary requests would start coming in from all 116 agencies. The big ones would be the hospitals — generally more than two hundred pages long — and the child-care agencies. Every request had to be analyzed and some consensus reached.

Early in February, Joe Willen and I would go downtown to the Hanover Bank for a large loan to keep Federation going until fund raising got under way. It would be made simply on our signatures, and since neither of us was very rich it was an acknowledgment by the bank that Federation was here to stay.

Then consultations with the fund-raising people: How much do they expect to raise this year? Four of us would commence budget work. I'd go out to lunch at 12:30, usually with a potential big donor.

The budget process was a three-month affair that culminated in hearings commencing late in March and continuing through May. Usually I left the office at 7:00 P.M. — but not necessarily for home. As a rule I was out three or four nights on business. Only Friday night was sacrosanct. I was putting in seventy-hour weeks. It could have been more if I had to attend Joe Willen's other social invention: working breakfasts for fund-raising efforts. Since I wasn't directly involved I could skip those. (You pay a price for those crazy working hours. When my daughter left for Sarah Lawrence College she said with some bitterness, "I don't know my father; I hardly ever see him.")

In mid-May the whole Budget Committee finalized grants and wrote its report for the Board of Trustees. At its June meeting the budget was voted, and the pressure would be off. That meant the Hexter family was free to vacation, generally at a little place I had at Saranac Lake, or travel.

In September the campaign would start. I'd help out in the fund raising. How? Take a heavy giver who wasn't too happy about some distribution. I'd have to show him how we arrived at that particular percentage and just what was involved. Somehow this process involved almost as many night meetings as in the fall. I was picked for this hand holding because everybody with serious money wants to talk to the boss, not an

Farewell Jerusalem, Hello New York

assistant assistant. Then there were the personal items: helping to get somebody's son into medical school; aged parents into a home for the aged; a daughter into a good hospital for her confinement. A Mr. Fix-It. A useful intermediary. All this was part of the job.

Not all requests were straightforward. One Rumanian immigrant, who had made a fortune here, had a wife and children — and a lady friend in Buenos Aires. He wanted to help his friend, but his money here was tied up by the war. The man's lawyer came to me for help. I schemed a bit and in time we were able to help the lady in Argentina. The man was grateful and when he died there were some very precious bequests to Federation.

Another case involved the wife of a prominent, wealthy Federation donor. Her mental health was fragile and she had one peculiar whim. It involved a minor Federation agency to which we gave more than it would have gotten normally just to keep her happy — and functioning. When she died her husband acknowledged the debt to Federation with an outsize memorial gift.

Not until the summer of 1949 did I get a chance to visit the new state of Israel. My wife and I and some old friends from Boston toured the country. I had a joyful reunion with Avraham Hartzfeld, my closest friend, who was now a member of the Knesset and a revered figure in the new country as its great "village builder." He told me how our pride and joy, Be'er Tuvia colony, had kept the Arabs from getting at Tel Aviv during the 1948 war; how vital the stockade and watchtower program in the 118 settlements had been in keeping Arab invaders from overrunning them. We talked about our colleague Frederick Kisch, who in 1939 had gone back into the British army and risen to brigadier general as the chief engineer for General Montgomery's Eight Army in North Africa; how he was killed leading his men in defusing a Nazi mine field in 1943. Now a settlement, Kefar Kisch, and the Kisch Memorial Forest in lower Galilee were named after him. There were other deaths in the decade since the Hexters had left Palestine. Yehoshua Hankin, the legendary land purchaser who had acquired more than 150,000 acres for the new land, died in 1945; Judah Magnes, the great advocate of an Arab-Jewish state, died in 1948.

The great war of independence had been won and an armistice finally attained in January 1949. Israel had lost none of its old territory and had increased its land holdings by about half. It held a continuous stretch of land, including all of Galilee and a bridge reaching the New City of Jerusalem. Ben-Gurion had been elected prime minister by the dominant

Life Size

functions.

Near Wadi Ara, the historical route into Egypt from Mesopotamia, our car was stopped by a military vehicle. "Is Dr. Hexter here?" an officer asked. My first reaction was apprehension: What terrible thing happened? It turned out that Ben-Gurion, who was staying at a hotel in Tiberias, wanted to know if I could arrange to see him there that afternoon. We changed our schedule and went to the hotel.

The greetings were warm. He explained that he had gotten our itinerary from Hartzfeld and was anxious to see me before I left Israel. Why? He wanted me to become the new minister of welfare in his cabinet. I was stunned into speechlessness for a full minute. When I recovered I blurted out that I wasn't even a citizen of Israel. He shook his mane. A mere detail. "We'll make an exception for you."

In fact, citizenship was the least of it, as both of us knew. I had been the odd man out in the Executive for a decade. The non-Zionist, the one who had argued against statehood; the one who had refused to abide by strict party membership as the key to colonization or loans.

My first thought was, My God, what an opportunity! But I said, let me talk it over with my wife. And I did. I told her what a fantastic chance it would be to shape the welfare of a new nation, the ultimate dream of every social worker. But even as I stressed the pluses the minuses were ever present, like a persistent dark cloud.

Marguerite said she didn't want to go back to Israel. They had just been through one war and others were likely. The Arab neighbors were still militantly opposed to the new country. And I owed Federation. I had been there ten years, but the major portion of my work was still to come.

In the end I had to tell Ben-Gurion that I couldn't accept. But, I added, if I had been a bachelor nothing would have stopped me. It was one of those major forks in the road of life and I couldn't take the new path offered. Inevitably during the years ahead I would sometimes daydream of what my life would have been like if I had taken the cabinet post.

It took some effort to get back to work in September. All I could think of was the series of battles that would stem from the Distribution Committee's decisions; the inner feuds; the stroking necessary for some of our major givers. That was balanced by recalling some of the battles I had been in at the Jewish Agency Executive; the attacks on me, the non-Zionist; the constant vigilance; the revolvers; the guard dogs. Still, I was proud to have been asked. If no one else did, I knew that Ben-Gurion had fully appreciated my years in Palestine.

Farewell Jerusalem, Hello New York

9

The Mature Years

WARM PERSONAL relationships had been the key to much of my effectiveness in Palestine, and it was no different at Federation. Joe Willen had the infinitely tougher job of fund raising, so that I never had to *ask* anyone for money. I was guided by an English ethical maxim that a man's main role in life was the fulfillment of interest and the fullest development of capacities. If I could aim at that I didn't have to worry about finding a man's purse. Capture his mind, not his vanity.

What I embarked on was a developing process that went from acquaintanceship to friendship. You shared their problems with children, with family, even with business. You become a person they can talk to frankly without feeling that it's going to cost them one way or another. You helped where you could.

My close friendship with Leonard Block is a good example. I first spotted him on the board of the Hillside Hospital, a Federation agency. He was bright, well spoken, and clearly a man who did his homework. By then I knew a little of the family business, the Block Drug Company. It had been begun by his father, Alexander Block, a Russian immigrant who started a drugstore on Fulton Street in Brooklyn. He turned wholesaler in 1909 and by 1925 was in the drug-manufacturing business. Right up to his death in 1953 Alexander Block was buying small drug and dental-products firms. Under Melvin and Leonard Block's direction the firm had expanded greatly. Now it has 3,000 employees worldwide, with factories in several foreign countries. Now it also made insecticides, household cleansers, and even ethical pharmaceuticals.

134

A tall, attractive man, Leonard Block seemed like one of those near-future leaders that Federation had to attract. I invited him to join the Federation Board of Trustees and become a member of the Distribution Committee.

I had made it a policy not to get yes men on the committee; that's building on quicksand. In fact, I've always sought out people who rubbed me the wrong way intellectually, because out of that contest of will and concepts progress would emerge. But now I began to feel as if I introduced a roadblock into the committee.

Every committee member showed up for the Block-Hexter showdowns, which were sharp and to the point. We both won our fair share, but on one particular point about hospital finance I felt Leonard had gone too far, and I was upset. There was a frost in the relationship for a time.

One day I got a call from Abram L. Sachar, chancellor of the very new Brandeis University in Massachusetts. I was on the Board of Trustees, and had been helping line up major donors and detailed advice on how to approach others.

"Maurice, are you standing up?" I said, yes. "Well, sit down. This is going to floor you."

I sat down. He had just gotten a $10,000 check from Leonard Block, he told me — toward a chair that was being arranged in my name in the field of communal relationships. Abe knew of my current difficulties with Block, so both of us were mystified. I phoned the Block home and Leonard was away. His wife, Adele, got on the phone. I told her about the $10,000. Of course, she knew about our current feud at the Distribution Committee, since she was almost equally involved in the family's philanthropies. (The Blocks give away 50 per cent of their large annual income.)

She laughed. "That's his acknowledgment that he has to lose sometimes. That check was his admission that he's been taught a lesson. He considers it a payment for tuition."

You can't stay mad at a man like that! We became very good friends. He rose to chairmanship of the Distribution Committee for a five-year period. He was easily one of the most useful volunteers Federation ever developed.

He is also one of the very few people I've ever known who saw me speechless for two full minutes. (I was only speechless for *one* minute when Ben-Gurion made his offer in Israel.) This happened later, when Leonard was chairman of the Communal Planning Committee. We were working then on the problems of the Jewish Association for Services to

The Mature Years

the Aged (JASA). Leonard had worked out a plan that enabled us to tap federal, state, and city sources for JASA institutions. Still, we needed a lot of big private donations.

Leonard had persuaded the committee that services for the aged would have to be extended *outside* an institution; that we needed buildings with apartments for the aged who are still somewhat ambulatory. These apartments would have special bathrooms and kitchen facilities so that residents could live in them comfortably — and safely. Some $4 million was needed to get this project under way. He was counting on me to lead it. And he volunteered the first $500,000. Great — but there was still $3.5 million more to go.

I looked up at him. "Leonard, have I sold out too cheaply?"

He understood, and smiled. "No. We're fair game if you'll need more." Still, it would be unfair to ask the Blocks to foot the *whole* bill.

A few weeks later a good friend, Lewis Green, had been hospitalized at Mt. Sinai. He was a major Wall Street operator and since his friend, Gus Levy, was president of the hospital Lew Green's private room had the only stock ticker at the hospital that week. (Gus was sure the ticker presence would expedite the friend's convalescence.) After we chatted a while Lew Green said he was particularly glad I had come by because he had a question for me. About a year earlier his wife had undergone major surgery at the hospital and he vowed then if she emerged successfully he would do something in gratitude. What could I suggest? So I pulled out the material Leonard Block had gotten together on the JASA proposal, and added that the Blocks had started the ball rolling with a gift of half a million dollars.

He said that was a great coincidence, because apartments for the aged were something he too had been thinking about, but that he'd first like to talk about it to his doctor, Lester Tuchman (the husband of historian Barbara Tuchman). I talked to Dr. Tuchman and he too liked the idea. Since he was also the Block family doctor I had high hopes.

We fixed a date to visit the Greens at their apartment at 1100 Park Avenue. Leonard Block came in especially for this from his country place in Elberon, New Jersey. When we got to the apartment house the doorman told us the Greens had gone out. I was awfully embarassed because Leonard had made a special trip. When I got home I got a frantic call from Lewis Green. He was terribly apologetic: He had forgotten the appointment, and asked us to come by the next day. I called Leonard and asked him to come in again, and added that Green's guilt about missing the appointment might help us.

On New Year's Day we went again to the Green apartment and I outlined the program. He asked us to excuse them while they discussed our request for $1 million. While we were waiting Leonard and I got a little nervous. Had we asked too much? Should we have been content with a $500,000 gift?

After five minutes Lewis Green came back and said firmly, "Look, we've talked it over and we won't give you a million." Leonard and I looked at each other: Yes, we should have asked for less. Lewis Green continued: "No, we'll give you two million." I was speechless for *two* minutes. That's how we got the great JASA program off the ground, with apartment houses built especially for the ambulatory aged. Thanks to Leonard Block, I got memorialized in the project: When the Hebrew Union College Seminary in the West 60s became available Leonard offered $750,000 to convert them, provided they carried the names of Maurice and Marguerite Hexter. And so they do.

When World War II was over Federation plunged into an extraordinary building fund for expansion, modernization, and research. We knew that the world was going to be different; that every old assumption now needed reexamination. Clearly in the new age we could no longer base our prime fund-raising on the old "Our Crowd," the rich German-Jewish families. Those Federation stalwarts were dying off and some of their offspring no longer had Jewish interests. Clearly there were going to be huge population shifts. Veterans were getting great incentives to acquire their own homes in the suburbs, where Federation hadn't ventured before. For the first time Federation planned a voluntary hospital from the ground up: Long Island Jewish Hospital, on the border between Queens and Nassau County, outside the city. (In its first year of operation, 1955, the hospital served 55,000 patients.)

There was also an extended look at leisure-time activities other than at Y buildings. The Henry Kaufman Campgrounds opened in 1953 in Long Island, Staten Island,* and Rockland County—the first rural day camps in the New York area with permanent structures and facilities. (Some twenty-five thousand children use these facilities every summer day.)

For all these major shifts there were still some major bedrock donors from the past to be counted on. These included Henry and Lucy Moses, who were among the most generous givers Federation ever had. He was

*The land the Henry Kaufman Foundation once bought for $160,000 is now being acquired by New York State for conservation purposes for some $24 million. The Day Camp is allowed to use the area for ninety-nine years.

The Mature Years

born in 1880 to a poor family in Scranton, Pennsylvania. He won a scholarship to Yale, graduated Phi Beta Kappa, and went on to Columbia Law School. He worked for a Jewish law firm and met Lucy Goldschmidt, whose father had founded the Public National Bank & Trust Company. It catered to the new immigrants and was run well enough to survive the Depression. On the morning after their marriage Lucy gave Henry a check for half her own sizable assets. She said, "Henry, I don't want to have more than you. Here's your share."

With capital of his own Henry Moses was able to found his own law firm, Moses & Singer, which is still one of New York's important law partnerships.

He also gambled a bit—on oil wells. In those early days it was easier to hit a producing well, and Henry Moses soon became quite wealthy. He became president of his father-in-law's bank and built it up. In 1956, after he had a stroke, Henry Moses arranged the merger of the family bank—the Moses family now controlled most of its stock—into the Bankers Trust Company. Instead of cash he elected to take stock in Bankers Trust. As a result the Moses family became the leading stockholder in Bankers Trust.

I had gotten to know the Moses family shortly after I joined Federation. For one thing he was one of our steadiest contributors, at least $100,000 a year. He was also a mainstay of Montefiore Hospital, which he served as president from 1936 to 1948, and probably the major factor in converting it from a nursing home to a major hospital for chronic diseases. There was nothing the hospital needed that he didn't personally finance. In addition, he and his wife put up the large laboratory building, for $7 million.

Oddly enough, Lucy Moses became a friend of Mme. Marie Curie, who together with her husband, Pierre, won the Nobel Prize for physics in 1903 for their work in radium and radioactivity—and then another Nobel Prize, in chemistry, in 1911. (She was the first Nobel "repeater.") In 1910 Marie Curie, a stubborn and rather difficult person, came to the United States, and Lucy befriended her. Pierre Curie had been killed in a Paris street accident. Lucy was instrumental in putting together a fund of $100,000 to acquire a gram of radium as a gift by American women to this heroine of science. The two women exchanged many letters, which Lucy published after Mme. Curie died in 1934.

After Henry Moses had a partially disabling stroke in 1956 I visited him every week. He assumed that he wouldn't be around too much longer and in anticipation he planned to leave everything to his wife. He did that, he once told me, because then she would have lots of attendance — and attendants.

When he died in 1961 Lucy Moses remained Bankers Trust's largest single stockholder. She stayed on in their magnificent duplex on Fifth Avenue and I kept up my weekly visits. She continued the large contributions to Montefiore until a freeze developed, over a social gaffe. At a Montefiore fund-raising dinner someone put Lucy Moses at a distant rear table, and it looked for a time as if the Moses benefactions to the hospital might cease. (The seating arrangment was only part of the problem: The hospital's new director may have felt that he had to end the heavy Moses influence at the institution.)

As it happened, the frost on an old relationship came at a time when Joe Willen and I were seeking very large sums from very rich people for the most expensive educational venture Federation had ever gotten involved in: the Mt. Sinai Medical School. Mrs. Moses was still furious at the slight and I sought to redirect her interest to another hospital. I persuaded her to give the medical school project $9 million, plus another $11 million to the hospital itself.

In time peace was made and Lucy Moses again became a major Montefiore contributor.

The creation of the Mt. Sinai Medical School deserves a volume by itself, perhaps written by a gifted novelist, a modern Trollope. At one point, for example, there was a sensible compromise being considered: that there should be one new medical school, not two. For Montefiore Hospital also was out to create a medical school, Einstein. But the effort — which would have saved about $200 million, I think — collapsed because of the personal rivalries of two big givers.

In the end both schools were created. Tens of millions were donated to Mt. Sinai Medical School by Joe Klingenstein, his brother-in-law, Milton Steinbach, Gus Levy, and the Annenberg family, which gave $15 million. And Lucy Moses. (I was intimately involved and in 1979 the Mt. Sinai Medical School gave me an honorary doctorate. It really should have been an advanced degree in midwifery.)

Federation took the position from the start that it would not support the Mt. Sinai Medical School, except for the full-time specialists we had authorized back in 1939 when Leo Arnstein first brought that problem to my attention. So today the school is supported separately. Inevitably there is competition between Federation and the school for the big givers' purses.

There were other problems for Mt. Sinai, particularly finding a university sponsor, which was necessary to satisfy medical authorities and to get a $26 million grant from the federal government for construction of the main building. At one point, after Columbia and Princeton had bowed out, I was deeply involved in trying to get Brandeis to become the sponsor. I had been close to Abe Sachar, its founder, from the start, and had been helpful to him in many ways.

For a time it looked as though the affiliation would go through smoothly, but out of nowhere came an obstacle — one that I had helped develop decades before. It was Beth Israel Hospital, which I had been instrumental in relocating next to the Harvard Medical School when I was director of the Boston Federation. I had directed the hospital toward its present preeminent stage and now it was standing in the way of a merger between Brandeis and Mt. Sinai Medical School. I had to come down from my Saranac summer home one day to take part in a Brandeis board meeting to decide the issue. I could see that a large number of Boston members feared that if such a connection were established Beth Israel Hospital would be hurt, or at least diminished. By a split vote the Brandeis board rejected the affiliation. I think they still regret it because they would have gotten Brandeis a strong alumni representation throughout the United States with a Mt. Sinai nexus. Over the past eighty-five years Mt. Sinai has given fine clinical training to many doctors who went south and west. Being good practitioners, they become prominent and successful citizens in their communities. They become, in effect, excellent solicitors, because their patients are grateful.

Eventually Mt. Sinai worked out an affiliation with City University of New York (the Albert Einstein College of Medicine joined Yeshiva University). There were lots of problems, particularly on top staff appointments to the hospital, which must have the approval of the medical school. Mt. Sinai always had rigorous procedures before appointing and at one point we faced a delicate problem. The appointment of a surgeon, Dr. Percy Klingenstein, was being considered. As it happened his brother, Joe Klingenstein, who was on the board (and a major contributor) said, "If my brother is appointed, I'll resign." Why? "I know he's a very able surgeon but he's my brother, and Mt. Sinai must not only be right but must be seen to be right. If my brother got the job, even if he's the best man for the job, it wouldn't *seem* right." The Hospital for Joint Diseases grabbed his brother.

As I said, there's a marvelous novel here.

The sixties was a time of really large contributions to Federation, to Mt. Sinai Medical School and many other institutions. A new generation of multimillionaires — few of them of German-Jewish stock — had been created. Lots of private businesses were encouraged to go public, because there were many Wall Street firms seeking to make the profitable conversions. If a man's business yielded him a million a year he could probably go public and get $20 million for the business. Often in cash. Others had the right touch at the right time. Joe Mailman and his brother, two bright Jewish boys from Utica, New York, dove happily into razor-blade manufacture, in competition with mighty Gillette, which gave them a lot of trouble. They sold out at the right time and invested with great acumen in New York real estate, to become very wealthy. Both became very generous donors.

So now in the sixties we had a new generation of big givers that needed cultivation. They made possible the great growth of Federation in that decade as well as the spread of our agencies to Nassau and Suffolk and to Westchester — in effect, a Greater New York Federation instead of one limited to the five boroughs. I suspect we shall never see such a great spurt again. At least, I won't.

The enormous giving to Jewish causes naturally aroused interest elsewhere. Universities and museums and cultural centers began paying attention to these big givers, such as Larry Wien, a New York lawyer who had grown enormously wealthy through real-estate syndication, which he more or less founded. He would spend every Wednesday on Federation matters when he was president, from 1960 to 1963. Columbia University, where he had attended college and law school, began courting him after discovering he had given Brandeis about $15 million. He soon joined the Columbia University Board of Trustees. Eventually he put up all the money to build Columbia's Wien Stadium, replacing its old Baker Field. At the same time he became one of the major donors at Lincoln Center.

In 1967 I was seventy-six and Joe Willen was seventy. It was time to make way for younger men. Walter Mendelsohn, a wealthy New York attorney who was president of the Jewish Board of Guardians and a major contributor, was on the search committee for replacements. He said it was a tough search because "we've got to find another son of a bitch like you, Maurice." He added that he hoped I didn't mind his speaking frankly. I said I didn't mind, but why "a son of a bitch?"

"You tell us what's on your mind even though you know we don't like to hear it. That's a service. There aren't too many men around in the field with that ability."

Pension arrangements were finally worked out for Joe and myself, which was possible because I had created the first pension scheme at Federation. I felt it necessary if social work was to become a profession. We had made great strides in using our agencies as training areas for new generations of social workers, just as hospitals train interns and residents. Such trained but salaried professionals had a right to expect financial arrangements for their later years.

Federation decided to give us a big send-off. More than a thousand men and women attended the affair at the Waldorf-Astoria on January 19, 1967, which was "disguised" as a monthly meeting of the Board of Trustees of Federation. The occasion was also the fiftieth anniversary of the founding of Federation, on January 10, 1917. There were lots of speeches and encomiums from all over, including the Pope, who sent the head of the Pro Deo Free International School of Social Studies in Rome. The Pope praised "the beneficial activities developed by the Messrs. Maurice Hexter and Joseph Willen. . . . The Holy Father is pleased because of the precious work you have accomplished for so many good organizations."

Louis Lefkowitz, deputized for an ailing Governor Rockefeller, called us "two men unique in the annals of philanthropy. . . . They've distributed over one and a half billion dollars for humanity. . . . They have erected for Federation an enormous and solid base to build for the future." Mayor Lindsay added that Federation had done one of the most incredible jobs in private philanthropy anywhere in the world.

For me the most moving words came from Edward M. M. Warburg, Felix's son. He said: "My father had a genius for choosing good men, and he chose Maurice Hexter."

The most amusing comments came from the venerable Judge Joseph Proskauer. He called us "the greatest double-header that ever played on the field of philanthropy." He said Joe would have made a great dentist, one practiced in painless extraction. "You not only take money from us but we thank you for being permitted to give."

The time came for us to respond to the plaudits. Joe called me "that tough-minded giant among us . . . the architect of the modern Federation." He went on to delineate our "Odd Couple" relationship we had for twenty-eight years. "We had our disagreements and fights but we always returned to a good working relationship. Like the bitter comment of a harried wife: *"Kill* him, yes! *Divorce* him, never!"

Now that I could sculpt full time, I joked, I was still in the game of chiseling. I alluded to the fact that I had probably antagonized many prominent Federation board members at one time or another with Distribution Committee decisions. "They all suffer from equal distribution of injustice." My wife and daughter, I said, had had to "pay a price for my communal services. . . . I hope they think it was all worthwhile."

There was lots of handshaking afterward in the Astor Gallery and I assured a few old-timers that I'd no longer be on top but on tap, for Federation had signed us on as consultants, with separate office space in a suite at 57th Street and Madison Avenue.

It had been a grand evening, far less dolorous and dire than my leave-taking of the Executive of the Jewish Agency in Palestine. But this was my last parting with an organization.

There had been a more personal, and much tougher, leave-taking three years before, when I was seventy-three. A friend and I got into a cab headed for home after dinner when he said, "You know how many cigarettes you've smoked since dinner?" I didn't. "You've smoked exactly two packs, or forty cigarettes." I couldn't believe him. He said he had counted in horrified fascination. He looked at me with a small smile. "I'll bet you $100 you can't stop smoking for the next two weeks." I took the bet and that was my last smoke. I never got lung cancer, but there were some sequelae. Later, X-rays revealed that I did have a lung disease—water accumulating in the lining of my lungs. The therapy was inserting a long needle into the lung through my back and tapping the water out. I think Dr. Alvin Teirstein took out a quart. After he finished I thanked him and kidded: "Well, I used to be on top and now I'm just on tap."

At our "consultant" retirement offices we pretty much went our own ways. I quickly converted the place into a sculpture studio. Joe Willen had no such outlet. The death of his wife, Pearl, in 1968, had pulled him down greatly. Later he married the daughter of Ira Younker, a wealthy executive who retired early from the department store business to devote much of his time to the Jewish Family Service. He and his wife had two children. The first, a boy, was somewhat handicapped, so Ira concentrated on his daughter, Janet. She later became a champion golf player, just as her father had been.

One of the long-term feuds at the upper levels of Federation had been between Ira Younker and my old friend Dr. Harry Friedman. When Younker had to mention Harry in a report or memo he would use lower case letters, "h" and "f," to indicate his "contempt." He was childish in other ways, too, but he did make some signal and useful changes in the Jewish Family Service's direction. All of us were appalled when he left no money to Federation in his will, let alone to his favorite, the Jewish Family Service. A curious case.

When I left Federation the president was Buddy Silberman, one of a

The Mature Years

long line of extraordinary Jewish leaders beginning with Felix Warburg. Buddy had something extra. He was probably the most dedicated layman I ever met. At one time I even urged him to give up his position as president to succeed me professionally in Federation. He thought about it, but decided that he'd be no good taking a salary: He was born to be a volunteer. (I had known his grandfather, head of Consolidated Cigar, who was one of the meanest people I've ever encountered. Buddy was everything his ancestor wasn't: warm, intelligent, generous.)

He became the prime donor of a special project I had long been interested in: the Hunter College School for Social Work. His $4 million gift made it possible for the school to grow to the point where it gives M.A.s and doctorates. By a curious coincidence, the building the school is now housed in is the one in which Buddy was born.

After retirement my routine changed so that I majored in sculpture and minored in philanthropy. Some of it was indirect, but effective nevertheless.

For many years I've lunched on Saturdays at the Harmonie Club at a table with Leonard Block, Joe Mailman, Leon Hess, Max Som, Eli Ellis, Julian Bach, and Jack Rudin. There's so much wealth around that table that even I, with my $30,000 pension and occasional sculpture sales, can't depress the annual income average very much. At lunch I'd often mention some interesting development I'd heard about at a Federation agency. Once I talked enthusiastically about a new hyperbaric oxygenation chamber I heard about from a doctor at Mt. Sinai. Apparently it was not only a perfect cure for the bends and for gangrene but it had great promise for arresting strokes if caught early. I was quite enthusiastic. A few weeks later I heard from my source at Mt. Sinai. He was a bit giddy: He had just received a $2 million check from Leon Hess to apply toward further research on use of the chamber for strokes.

My retirement entailed two obligatory foreign trips a year. In 1950 I had been elected a director of ICA (the Jewish Colonization Association), which I had helped redirect toward contributing its great funds toward Palestine. Now it was a steady and generous donor to Israeli agricultural efforts. I was the first American director, which meant that every April and September I had to fly to Paris or London to attend the semiannual board meeting.

Late in May I'd go up to Saranac for my summer stay. I had discovered the place the summer Sidney Pritz of Cincinnati brought me up with him to act as chaperone for his lovely guest, Alma Gluck, the opera singer.

Life Size

I fell in love with the place and wanted to get back to it. The chance came after the Hexters returned to New York from Palestine.

At that time the lower end of the lake was almost completely Jewish. There were the "camps"– splendid summer homes – of Adolph Lewisohn, Jules Bache, the Goldmans, and the Seligmans. The northern end was occupied by the Saranac Inn, where Jews were not accepted. The inn was so anti-Semitic it wouldn't even permit Governor Lehman to play on the golf course. In time the inn changed hands and was opened to Jews. I think I was one of the first guests. After a couple of summers I bought the place I now have and generally go up there from the Middle of May until mid-September (It isn't winterized).

There were Hexter family developments, good and bad. Marjorie, born in a Catholic hospital in Milwaukee and raised in a sometimes dangerous Palestine, graduated from Sarah Lawrence and taught prekindergarten for a few years.

My daughter's first marriage to A. Jacob Abrams, an attorney who eventually gave up private practice and applied his legal training to several business projects where I hear he has had success, ended in divorce. Their union produced two children, Terry Ann and John M., both of whom give me much joy. Terry had her Doctorate in Psychology and is on the staff of the Kaiser Memorial Hospital in San Jose, California. John has his Doctorate in Molecular Biology from Stanford and continues his post-doctoral work at MIT.

Marjorie's remarried to Howard M. Cohen, a prominent attorney with an outstanding record at Harvard Law School. He is with a well-known New York firm with a full service practice. He, too, had two children from a previous marriage. Jonathan has his M.D. from Pennsylvania and additional degrees in allied subjects at Stanford and is now on the faculties of Carnegie-Mellon and Pittsburgh. Tamara, a graduate of Tufts, is just finishing a promising novel about a Nepali and American family. They also give me great joy. The four children are very close to each other, which has been a blessing. They have a very good relationship with me.

Shortly after my retirement Marguerite developed osteoporosis, that all-too-common malady of older women. Inevitably it led to falls and broken hips, which meant that she had to get about with a walker. Her last years were painful ones. She died in 1979. We had been married fifty-eight years, and considering my introspective qualities and sometimes workaholic habits it had been a very good marriage.

Shortly after came the death of my brother, Leo, who was four years older. He died at 91. He had led a troubled life, punctuated by bouts of

The Mature Years

heavy drinking and gambling. Eventually he did get a college degree and I was able to help him get a job in social work. My sister, Betty, the youngest, went to the University of Cincinnati as I did, got a degree, married and taught for many years in the local schools. She died at the comparatively youthful age — for the Hexters anyway — of eighty-four.

My routine since Marguerite's death has been fairly constant. I get to my studio-office at Federation — only a block and a half from my apartment — in the morning and sculpt. There are phone calls to and from friends to chat, exchange gossip. Often I'll lunch out with old friends from Federation days. As a rule my big meal is luncheon. For supper I seldom have more than a bowl of soup and some bread. I have a housekeeper who comes in three times a week to take care of the apartment and laundry.

I've always been an avid reader, but recently glaucoma has made that pleasure more difficult. I watch some TV but because of my hearing have to turn it up full blast, like some teenager trying out his hi-fi equipment.

Most Friday afternoons are devoted to a visit to someone who is even older than I am — Lucy Moses, who at 102 is doubtless one of the wealthiest centenarians on earth. She lives in the huge apartment with a large household staff. She is also an extraordinarily generous woman, and often during my visits will ask me, "Maurice, what useful work can I do in this or that area?" And I make suggestions.

A few years ago she decided that instead of honoring friends after her death she'd make large donations to them now. She allotted $2 million each to Dr. Arthur M. Fishberg, her physician, and to me. "You pick out the agencies you want to give the money to." Each of us was an instant Maecenas! It is a lovely feeling, giving away money to good causes. My largest single contribution, $350,000, was to the Hebrew Home for the Aged in Riverdale, which I had helped much earlier through my resolution of the Stettenheim affair. But then my help had been through maneuver and cunning, rather than raw money, as now. Quite a different feeling.

The Home impressed me because it was the least institutional agency I ever had anything to do with. There was no institutional smell and, most unusual, you couldn't bribe a staff member. They take the aged who are at least partially ambulatory, not the totally bedridden. With a $21 million gift from Henry Kaufman they've set up a pavilion for Alzheimer victims. The Home has several of my pieces, including one life-size rendition of an aged woman, *Senior Citizen*.

I made other "gifts" this way — some $25,000 to Harvard; $100,000 to Mt. Sinai Hospital, $200,000 to the Block-Hexter Camp, $50,000 to the National Sculpture Society.

Life Size

The great surprise at such a nice large gift from an unlikely source — me — made the powers at the Home decide they'd do something in return. In May 1989 they gave me a ninety-eighth birthday party at the Harmonie Club. With something called Nostalgia Video there was a large-screen panorama of people and places in a long life — a faded, sepia world I had once inhabited vigorously. Well, the least I could do to thank them for a lovely party was to provide my juniors — *everyone* present was my junior — with some first-hand observations: *How to know you are growing older.* Among them:

The gleam in your eye is from the sun hitting your bifocals.
Your little black book contains only names ending in M.D.
You know all the answers but nobody asks the questions.
You have too much room in the house and not enough in the medicine chest.
Your back goes out more than you do.

I once heard an amusingly cynical little sequence in London as a guide to a barrister's progress: *Get on, get honest, get honors.* You'd have to modify that considerably for social workers, because it's simply not a profession you can get rich in — so there isn't any incentive not to be honest in the first place. Still, there is a terminal resemblance. Honors to come — if you survive long enough, haven't made too many enemies, and have been able to get useful jobs done. And in our society, without the Queen's Birthday List, the commonest form of honor is the honorary degree.

There is always some amused cynicism among fund raisers when discussing honorary degrees. A standard trade quip is, "Colleges are built by degrees." And indeed, many colleges and universities owe much of their growth to the commencement-day pas de deux of giver and receiver. In recent years there has arisen another class of honorary degree recipients: the famous, who are enticed for a commencement address in return for an honorary degree. A clear enough trade. But the final category is less well known and arises when the university has been rendered a considerable voluntary service. Thus it happens that I, never a rich man, and certainly never possessing great fame, am the recipient of six honorary degrees. All earned, so to speak.

My first was from Brandeis in 1961, when I was a very youthful seventy. I had been helpful to its president, Abe Sachar, in many ways, but the most important probably was the guidance and suggested donors in getting the Heller School for Advanced Studies in Social Science under way.

The Mature Years

Yeshiva University came through a year later because I had been "of material help," as the lawyers put it, in getting them started with what is now the Wurzweiler School of Social Work.

The University of Santo Domingo came next, in 1975. Mainly, I suppose, in memory of the work I had done in helping get the Sosua colony of Jewish refugees under way back in 1940. The colony and its Jewish residents had helped enrich the island considerably.

In 1980 my old alma mater, the University of the State of Ohio at Cincinnati, joined the parade. For past services to the Jewish community of that city? Or possibly on the theory that if three universities had given me an honorary degree I surely must be worthy of another one. Maybe they were just proud of one of their oldest alumni.

Mt. Sinai Medical School in 1983. For decades I had been very attentive to the hospital's needs and helped introduce in 1939 the historic first of three full-time medical specialists, in spite of much medical opposition. Later, there was a very active role in helping get the Medical School under way, as far as Federation was concerned. And, I suspect, the fact that, by accident, I was able to get Mrs. Henry Moses interested, very strongly, in the hospital and medical school.

Hebrew Union College in 1988. Maybe it was their surprise at finding that I, a minor figure in their archives, was still around. There may be another factor: While I was in charge of the United Hebrew Charities in Cincinnati I was the first to expose the reform rabbinical students to the many aspects of Jewish community problems. In fact I was the first lecturer they ever had on the subject. I kept it up for six years.

Even institutions that couldn't give honorary degrees found ways to honor services rendered. In 1980 the Jewish Association for Services to the Aged (JSSA), to which I had long been partial, dedicated the Marguerite M. and Maurice B. Hexter Building at its center in New York. And sometimes you get honored, in part, because you're a good and successful patient. In 1988 I was honored at Mt. Sinai Hospital with the establishment of the Dr. Maurice Hexter Professorship in Medicine (Pulmonary). It could have been, of course, their enormous surprise that a chain smoker of more than fifty years — recently reformed, to be sure — was still around and that all he needed was some surgery by Dr. Alvin Teirstein, who is the head of the Division of Pulmonary Medicine. He probably saved my life. The chair was underwritten by my old friends Adele and Leonard Block.

There are other parts of me scattered around Mt. Sinai. The hospital has six of my sculptures, including busts of some of their greatest benefac-

Life Size

Maybe it's time to talk of my hobby of nearly forty years.

In 1950, when I was fifty-nine, I began musing on what a partially deaf person with absolutely no hobbies does after retirement. I never was a collector and while I enjoy travel, Marguerite and I had already done quite a bit of *that*. In any case, it wasn't something you could do all the time. During this on-again, off-again introspection my eyes lit on a clay head that Margie had done during a summer session at the University of Wisconsin. For some reason it suddenly struck my fancy. One possible reason: When I doodled it was always three-dimensionally, which is not common.

How do you go about learning to model in clay? You get a teacher, of course. As it happened, one of the Federation leaders at the time, Richmond Proskauer, had a daughter who was a sculptor. I asked, feeling a bit foolish, if his daughter, Nancy Dryfoos, did any teaching. She did, and eventually I went down to her studio on lower Third Avenue. I amused myself by noting I was trying to repair a gap in my education. Most kids start fooling around with clay in kindergarten, but since I never went to kindergarten. . . . Obviously, it was time to catch up.

Nancy Dryfoos started me in clay modeling. I picked it up reasonably well, but I wasn't happy with clay. After three months I told her I wanted to work in stone. She thought I was crazy: It took years of training before you could do any kind of creditable work in stone. There was no point in telling her I didn't have those years. For some morbid reason I kept thinking that after sixty I wouldn't be around long. No logic: Everyone in my family lived far longer than that.

As it happened there was some reinforcement for my hunch that I really wanted to work in stone. In 1948 I had become president of the Dominican Republic Settlement association (DORSA), and I had to make official visits there every year during my vacation time from Federation. While I was wandering around the island during one visit I came across an Italian sculptor working in stone. He was there because Trujillo felt that the marble deposits of his country should become better known. Since he always believed in direct action – good and bad – he imported three Italian experts to exploit the deposits. One of them was the sculptor.

He was generous with his time. He showed me the various tools – hammers, points, chisels, rifflers – used in working with stone, even permitted me to work in one of the studios. My early works weren't very good but I fell in love with the process. I felt a marvelous inner peace carv-

The Mature Years

ing stone. I had found the answer: This was what I would do in retirement. Meanwhile, I could chisel away — and in time drill away — in my spare time. How lucky I was, comparing myself with several Federation donors I knew who seemed to waste away when they retired.

Stone sculpture *endures*, my Italian friend pointed out, which can't be said of bronze, for example. Bronze was frequently melted down for weapons in time of war. As my work improved he suggested that perhaps when I had a chance I ought to visit his native city, Pietrasanta, where there was a remarkable school. (Michelangelo worked there and even opened his own quarry.) Now I try to get there at least once a year and work in a small studio I've rented. Since then I've worked in sandstone, black Belgian marble, and two types of granite, as well as onyx from Pakistan, Turkey, and the Argentine. Each produces different effects of light and shadow and, in the case of onyx, an additional quality of translucence.

I didn't formally retire from Federation until I was seventy-six, when to my surprise I was still spry and functioning. Sculpting is a lonely occupation and even that fitted in perfectly with my tendency toward inward isolation endured by those of us who have had hearing loss. If I had been born Catholic I suspect I would have ended in a Trappist monastery.

In time friends, family, and associates accepted the fact that I was serious about sculpture. After all, I had never displayed any facets of an artistic temperament. Maurice an *artist*?

There may be other, mysterious factors involved. Napoleon once said, "Were I not a conqueror, I would like to have been a sculptor."

When I won the gold medal at the National Sculpture Association annual show a lot of people realized that I had moved out of amateur, hobby status. I was a *sculptor*. This was reinforced when I won another gold medal at the 1979 annual show, for a larger-than-life-size stone bust of Egyptian President Anwar Sadat. It was purchased by the Aspen Institute for Humanistic Studies. I wrote Sadat after the prize announcement: "I began this bust the day after you announced your intended visit to Israel. I and myriad of others were electrified by your bold step which bodes so well and so much for so many. You have by this initiative changed an historic course from spears to plowshares. . . . May good health and inner peace constantly attend you."

Life Size

In his reply Sadat congratulated me for this "appreciation of the peace efforts. . . . This masterpiece reflects your spirit as a highly sensitive artist who understands and appreciates every sincere effort exerted for achieving genuine stability and tranquility for mankind." Inevitably, I mused on the possibly changed course of history if there had been such a determined and forceful peace leader of the Arabs when I was a member of the Executive of the Jewish Agency in Palestine.

10

Sculpture, A New Life

THE DIFFERENCE between the amateur and the professional sculptor is that the former wants to hold on to all his work, while the latter wants to sell it. But holding on to all my work became impossible physically, and in time I began selling some pieces or giving them to friends.

Some works resulted from challenges. Once, before I retired from Federation, Larry Wien was president. He was a hardheaded but extraordinarily generous donor to Federation and to Brandeis University. He looked at one of my pieces and said: "Maurice, there's something that's always puzzled me. Why is it that all the sculpture of a mother and child are pietistic, always of Mary and Jesus?" There was no good answer. "Tell you what," he suddenly said. "You make a mother and child who are *not* Mary and Jesus and I'll buy it."

I did — by turning the child's face toward the mother's back. He bought it, for twelve thousand dollars. This was the piece that won my first gold medal.

A few years later we met at a wedding — his granddaughter married my great-nephew. He asked me casually if I'd mind if he gave the sculpture away. I said, "No, you own it. But why are you giving it away?" It turned out that a grandson of his had been born recently at the New York University Medical Center and now Larry Wien wanted to do something for the center. He asked the dean to come over and said he'd like to do something for them in gratitude for the fine care his daughter and grandson had received there. "What would you like?" The dean looked around, spotted the mother-and-child sculpture, and said, "Give us that." I said, sure, give it to them.

Sculpture
a photographic portfolio

Granddaughter Terri unveiling Jenny *at Montefiore Hospital in 1960 as Victor Riesenfeld and Leon Fink look on. The sculpture is now at Brandeis University.*

Sculptor's Arm

1962
24"h. x 12"w. x 15"d.
Porphyry
Collection of the artist

Herbert Halweil photo

153

Candle Flame

1965
12"h. x 30"w. x 36"d.
Swedish granite
Collection of Brandeis
    Univeristy

Prophet

1970
27-½"h. x 15-¾"w. x 4¾"d.
Porphyry
Collection of the artist

Hexter with his Italian landlord in his studio at Pietrasanta, Italy circa 1970.

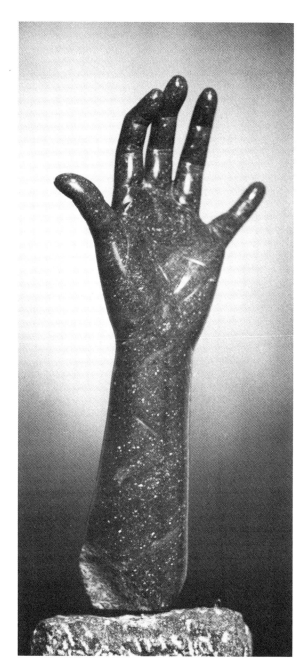

Arthritic Forearm

Ca. 1972
21-¼"h.
Porphyry
Hospital for Joint Diseases,
New York

157

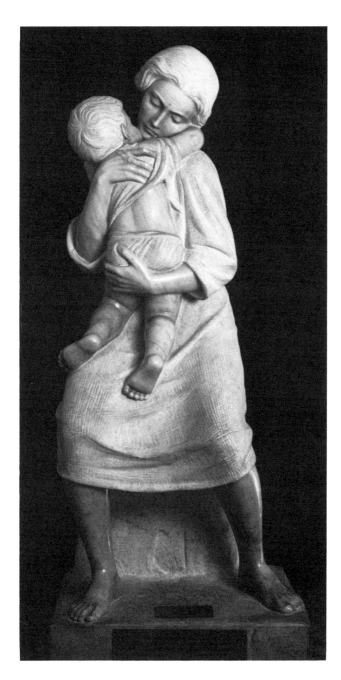

Mother and Child

1973
30"h. x 16-¾"w. x
  15"d.
Portuguese marble
Collection of New
    York University
    Medical School

Bird in Full Flight

1973
16"h. x 16"w. x 10-½"d.
Pakistan onyx on porphyry base
Collection of Mrs. Leon Hess

Carib Indian

Ca. 1975
17-½"h. x 11"w.
Pakistan onyx
Collection of the
    artist

Old Lady on Central Park Bench

Ca. 1975
Bas relief 22″h. x 15-½″ w.
Carrara marble
Collection of the late
    Lawrence Wien

160

Newsboy Asleep on Steps

1975
Bas relief 21″h. x 18″ w.
Porphyry
Collection of *The New York Times*

161

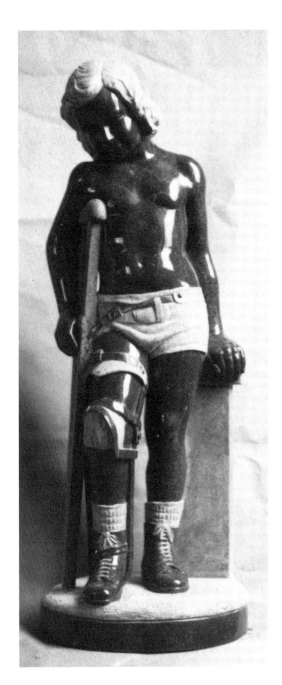

Handicapped Child

1976
35"h. x 10"w. x 13"d.
Porphyry
Collection of New York Society
   for Orthopedically
   Handicapped

162

Elderly Arab Shepherd

Ca. 1978
Bas relief 13-½″h. x 10-½″w.
Bardiglio Imperiale
Collection of Edward Rosenberg

Holocaust

1979
Bas relief 21-½"h. x 19-½"w.
Carrara marble
Collection of the Jewish Museum of
    New York

Chalutz (Pioneer)

1980
30"h. x 15"w. x 19"d.
Gray Norwegian granite
Collection of Mr. and Mrs. Leonard
    Block

Seal

1980
35-¼"h. x 29"w. x 18"d.
Black African granite on
   Wisconsin granite base
Collection of Mr. and Mrs.
   Leonard Block

166

Non Objective VI

1980
5' 11-½"h. x 4'7"w. x 15"d.
Swedish granite
Collection of the YMHA - Irene Kaufmann
   Settlement Center, Pittsburgh

Anwar El Sadat

1981
20"h. x 19"w. x 12"d.
Red Porphyry
Collection of Aspen Institute
for International Studies

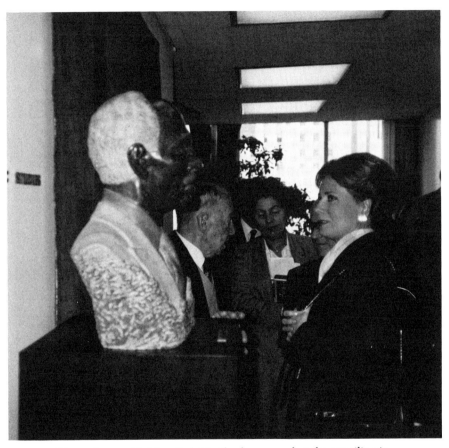

The sculptor with Mrs. Sadat in the foreground at the unveiling in
New York City in 1981.

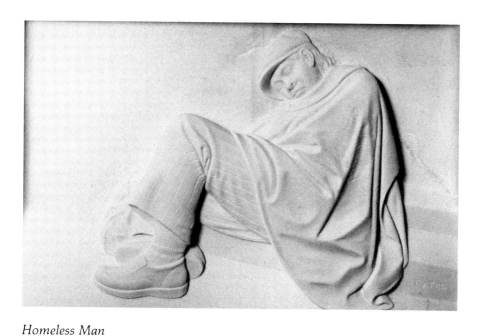

Homeless Man

1986
Bas relief 15-¾"h. x 25-½"w.
Carrara marble
Collection of Mr. and Mrs. Leon Hess

Two months later Larry phoned and asked me to give him the name of two sculpture appraisers. One rated the sculpture as worth $67,500 and the other at $75,000. Wien congratulated me on keeping way ahead of inflation with my sculptures.

Since then a number of my pieces have found their way into particularly appropriate settings. My *Sleeping Newsboy*, a three-dimensional translation of my very first professional report, "The Newsboys of Cincinnati," is in the board room of *The New York Times*. It is one of my great favorites, as it was Marguerite's.

My professional life in social work for six decades reinforced my concern about a certain drabness of all institutions, regardless of the efforts of dedicated trustees and decorators. I have been able to place a number of my pieces in hospitals, homes for the aged, community centers, and camps, where I like to believe they have brought solace at times to troubled people.

Scrubbed-up Surgeon, a life-size piece of Carrara marble, is at Montefiore Hospital. I promised to do it before some minor surgery — a hernia — by Dr. Leon Ginsberg. A propitiatory offer, I suppose. (Maybe I was still recalling the hostility of some surgeons when I helped Mt. Sinai introduce the concept of full-time chief surgeons.) *The Prophet*, in the Federation collection, was commissioned to stimulate legacies to Federation and its agencies by showing the bearded prophet symbolically writing names in a book. The Catholic Charities of New York has my *Mother and Child* in Italian porphyry and the Jewish Home and Hospital for the Aged has my life size *Old Lady*, inspired by the sublime dignity of one of its residents.

I didn't scant my own family. I did a fine piece, *Margie and Her Two Children*, which my daughter has in her apartment, and in *Motherhood* I caught a favorite pose of my mother in Dominican black marble.

And there were dues paid to my Palestine years in the form of the *Bust of Oriental Mountaineer*, in Italian porphyry. It portrays an Oriental Jew from the mountains of Iran I remembered who had come to Palestine and worked in the Galilee project to clear the fields of stones for large farming areas. Several of my pieces are at the Hebrew University in Israel. These include busts of Ben-Gurion, Dayan, Eban, and Elath. The Histadruth Building in Tel Aviv has a bust of my dear old friend Avraham Hartzfeld.

During most of the year I work in the offices Federation set aside for me as part of my retirement package, on the ninth floor of the Federation building in Manhattan. And from the end of May to mid-September I sculpt at my Saranac Lake summer home, where I work in a converted barn, or preferably in the open air. Long ago I learned to use the pneumatic drill — you should feel my right forearm — and high-speed buffers, which can change the crystalline surface and hence the color of marble. I even improvised a set of diamond-bit instruments which I've collected over the years from my dentist. (A fair number of *them* also became sculptors when they retire.)

From time to time I get commissions. A doctor I knew admired some of my work at a Harmonie Club exhibit and asked if I would do a head of his wife. I said yes and we agreed on a fee. When I finished it his wife and daughter admired it greatly, but when the physician joined them he looked it over for a minute or two and shook his head. Looking straight at his wife he said, "Dear, you're not that good-looking." He didn't want it. (I'd love to have tapes of the pillow talk at their apartment after *that* showdown.) He was a friend — I thought — and so I didn't go to court but simply took the head, which I still have in my New York studio.

How good is my stuff? Some of it, I think, is very good, and some is pretty bad. When I was eighty, in 1971, Leonard Block gave me a marvelous birthday party, which started with an exhibit of many of my works at the Whitney Museum, then on to the Carlyle Hotel for dinner. John Bower, director of the museum and a great authority on American art, in a warming little talk — I was warmed — called me a "gifted amateur whose works breathe the humanity of man himself." I was "not a great artist in the international sense," he said, but I had impressive technical skills.

A fair estimate, I think. Just as well that he gave me a modest appraisal, because several of the other speakers threw praise around with big ladles. Of me, not my sculpture. Bob Koshland, an old friend said with a rueful smile, "You've cost me a lot of money, Maurice, but you also taught me a great deal." And United States Circuit Court Justice Henry Friendly rekindled a memory I had almost forgotten — how we used to invite him frequently for dinner in Boston when he was a struggling student at Harvard Law School. In all, it was a most memorable evening, and even if only half of what they said was approximately true, it has been a pretty useful life. Or, as I put it in replying to the overflowing encomiums: "I've had a good run and I hope I've paid my dues. All of you know how to make a living, sometimes too good a living. And for some of you I've helped make a life. The trick was to make you have the courage of my convictions."

Sculpture, A New Life

A few years ago some good friends gathered about $300,000 to create the Hexter Sculpture Center at the Usdan Center for the Creative Arts, where young children from all parts of the city are given a chance to develop their talents. (Is there a self-mocking thought here? Imagine what you can do if you're young *and* talented instead of old, retired, and a very late starter?)

John Dryden, a sixteenth-century English poet and playwright known today primarily to graduate English students and to the occasional delver into books of quotations ("Men are but children of a larger growth" and "Beware the fury of a patient man") also wrote a poem that I've long cherished. In its own way it's a perfect coda for my own life:

> *Happy the man, and happy he alone,*
> *He, who can call to-day his own;*
> *He who, secure within, can say,*
> *(To-morrow, do thy worst, for I have liv'd to-day.)*
> *Be fair, or foul, or rain, or shine.*
> *The joys I have posses'd in spite of fates are mine.*
> *Not heav'n itself upon the past has pow'r;*
> *But what has been, has been, and I have had my*
> *hour.*

Index

Bureau of Immigration, 10

Cabot, Prof. Richard, 33, 36, 60
Calles, Plutarco, 38, 41
Campbell Soup, 6
Carlyle Hotel, 171
Carnegie Hall, 5
Carnegie-Mellon University, 145
Catholic Charities of New York, 170
Central Agricultural Council, 77, 99
Central Bank of Cooperatives, 53
Central Relief Committee, 41
Chancellor, Sir John, 76, 77
Chancellor, Sir John and Lady, 83
Chapultepec Park, 41
Children Astray, 33
Churchill Winston, 46, 91
Cicurels, 50
Cincinnati Inquirer, 7
Cincinnati & Ohio, 5
Cincinnati Post, 7
Cincinnati Times, 12
City College of the City University of
    New York, 11, 140
City Welfare Department of Children,
    127
Clifton College, 50
Cobra, 86
Cohen, Howard M., 145; illus., 27
Cohen, Dr. Jonathan, 145; illus., 28
Cohen, Judge A. K., 24
Cohen, Sir Leonard, 101
Cohen, Marjory and Howard, ix
Cohen, Tamara, 145; illus., 28, 30
Colonial Office, 79
Colonial Office in London, 81
Colonization Department, 90
Columbia University, 23, 48, 123, 140, 141
Columbia Law School, 138
Conference of Jewish Charities, 33
Congress of the World Zionist Organiza-
    tion, 111
Consolidated Cigar, 144
Coolidge, Pres. Calvin, 38
Cornell University, 35
Council of Jewish Federations and Wel-
    fare Funds, xii
Council of the Jewish Agency, 53, 54
Court Index, 6
Croix de Guerre, 49
Cummings, Nate, 149

Curie, Pierre, 138
Curie, Mme. Marie, 138
Cutler, Saul, 123

Dan family, 90
Dannenbaum, Mrs., 19
Davar, 77
Davenport, Marcia, 17
d'Avigdor-Goldsmid, Sir Osmond, 56, 65,
    96, 101, 113, 114, 126
Dawn O'Hara, 19
Day, Prof. Edmund Ezra, 35
Dayan, 170
Dayan, Moshe, 107
Dayan, Shmuel, 107
Dead Sea, 2, 105
de Hirsch, Baron Maurice, 100, 101
de Hirsch, Clara, 101
de Hirsch, Lucien, 100
Department of Economics, 37
Department of Preventive Medicine, 49
Department of Social Ethics, 33, 37
Deutsche Bank of Berlin, 47, 80, 96, 98,
    115
District Services Plan, 32
Division of Pulmonary Medicine, 148
Doar Hayom (Daily Post), 52
Dominican Republic Settlement Associa-
    tion, 124, 149
Donges Bay, 34
Driben, Saul, 128, 129
Drucker, Sol, 33
Dryden, John, 172
Dryfoos, Nancy, 149
Dzerzinsky, 44

Eban, 170
Edward VII, 100
Einstein, Albert, 34, 56
el Husseini, Haj Amin, 93
el Shawwa, Jamil Effendi, 93
Elath, 170
Elizabeth Inn, 109
Ellis, David, 24
Ellis, Eli, xi, 144
Emanuel, Alice, 103
Emergency Committee on Jewish Refu-
    gees, 38
Emergency Relief Fund, 79, 96, 99, 101,
    110, 113, 115
Emerson Hall, 37, 60; illus., 66

174

177

179

180

179

180

was designed by A. L. Morris.
The text was composed in Paladium
and printed by Knowlton & McLeary
in Farmington, Maine on Monadnock Caress.
The jacket and endleaves
were printed on Strathmore Grandee Text,
and the binding in Holliston Mills Roxite
was executed by New Hampshire Bindery
in Concord, New Hampshire.